T4-AFX-894

MAKING
REMARRIAGE
WORK

MAKING REMARRIAGE WORK

by

JEANNE BELOVITCH

Lexington Books

D.C. Heath and Company • Lexington, Massachusetts • Toronto

Grateful acknowledgment is made to the following for permission to reprint published materials:

"Hauntings," from the book *A New Marriage A New Life* by Frederic F. Flach, M.D., copyright 1978 by Frederic F. Flach. Used by permission.

"Vasectomy Reversal," by Jane Mickelson. This article was excerpted with permission from *Mothering Magazine*, volume 36, copyright 1985, published by Mothering Publications, P.O. Box 8410, Santa Fe, NM 87504.

"How to Choose a Surgeon," by Angie Pallow-Fleury, R.N. This article was excerpted with permission from *Mothering Magazine*, volume 36, copyright 1985, published by Mothering Publications, P.O. Box 8410, Santa Fe, NM 87504.

"The Experiences of Parents Who Share Custody," by Kathleen Walker, from the newspaper *The Ottawa Citizen*, copyright by *The Ottawa Citizen*. Reprinted by permission.

Library of Congress Cataloging-in-Publication Data

Making remarriage work.

Bibliography: p.
Includes index.
1. Remarriage—United States. 2. Family—
United States. 3. Remarried people—United States—
Family Relationships. I. Belovitch, Jeanne.
HQ536.M27 1987 306.8'4 86-45617
ISBN 0-669-14031-7 (alk. paper)
ISBN 0-669-14030-9 (pbk. : alk. paper)

Copyright © 1987 by G&R Publications, Inc.

All rights reserved. No part of this publication may be reproduced or transmitted in any form or by any means, electronic or mechanical, including photocopy, recording, or any information storage or retrieval system, without permission in writing from the publisher.

WIDENER UNIVERSITY
WOLFGRAM
LIBRARY
CHESTER, PA.

DISCARDED
WIDENER UNIVERSITY

Published simultaneously in Canada
Printed in the United States of America
Casebound International Standard Book Number: 0-669-14031-7
Paperbound International Standard Book Number: 0-669-14030-9
Library of Congress Catalog Card Number: 86-45617

The paper used in this publication meets
the minimum requirements of American National Standard
for Information Sciences—Permanence of Paper
for Printed Library Materials, ANSI Z39.48-1984.

87 88 89 90 91 8 7 6 5 4 3 2 1

To my mother and my father

Contents

Preface xv

Editor's Acknowledgments xix

1. A Look at Family Life, American Style 1

    More Than One Kind of Normal Family 1
    Lillian Messinger

    Reflections of a Family Court Judge 4
    Ernest Rotenberg

    Second Families Go Unprotected by the Law 7
    Donna Bilbrey

    Stepfamilies in England, France, and the
    Netherlands 9
    David A. Baptiste, Jr.

2. Is It Time to Remarry? 11

    Successful Marriages Are Renewed Marriages 11
    Frederic F. Flach, M.D.

    The Advantages and Challenges of Remarrying 13
    Frederic F. Flach, M.D.

    Love Is Not All . . . Success in Remarriage Requires
    Much More 15
    Paula Ripple Comin

    From "Never Again" to "I Do" 18
    Elizabeth Einstein

Are You Ready to Remarry? 20
Elizabeth Einstein

3.   The Cold Facts about Remarriage: Money, Prenuptial
     Agreements, and Wills 25

     Dare We Talk about Money? 25
     Claire Berman

     Is a Prenuptial Contract Necessary? 28
     Neal A. Kuyper

     A Look at Antenuptial Agreements 31
     Doris Jonas Freed

     Remarriage and Writing a Will 32
     Neal A. Kuyper

4.   Are You Prepared to Be a Second Wife? 37

     Being a Second Wife 37
     Donna Bilbrey

     A Second Wife, a Former Wife, and the Common
     Denominator 39
     Marie Kargman

     Fun in the Summer for Second Wives 41
     Donna Bilbrey

5.   Enriching Yourselves as a Couple 43

     How Does Sex Fare in Second Marriages? 43
     Frederic F. Flach, M.D.

     Do You *Both* Want a Child? 45
     Claire Berman

     How Not to Let Guilt Destroy a Second Chance 47
     Frederic F. Flach, M.D.

Denial Damages Chances for Successful Remarriage 49
Elizabeth Einstein

Are You Communicating? 51
Marie Kargman

Hauntings 54
Frederic F. Flach, M.D.

Facing the Feelings Remarriage Brings and Letting Go 57
Elizabeth Einstein

Vasectomy Reversal 62
Jane Mickelson

How to Choose a Surgeon 68
Angie Pallow-Fleury

6. Learning to Be a Stepparent 71

Coming to Terms in Stepfamilies: What to Call the
New Mom or Dad 71
Claire Berman

Stepping into Parenting Someone Else's Children 73
Patricia L. Papernow

How to Work with the Other Parents 80
Claire Berman

Guidelines for Stepfathers 83
Frederic F. Flach, M.D.

Unfulfilled Need or Malicious Intent? 86
David A. Baptiste, Jr.

Do Fathers Really Want Stepmothers to Influence
Their Children's Lives? 88
Frederic F. Flach, M.D.

How Parents Intensify Sexual Feelings between
Stepsiblings　91
David A. Baptiste, Jr.

7.　Strengthening Your New Family　95

Building a New Identity as a Stepfamily　95
Jamie Kelem Keshet

The Family in the Plain Brown Wrapper　98
Donna Bilbrey

"Where Do We Go from Here?"　99
Donna Bilbrey

Can a Social Contract Help Integrate a Stepfamily?　102
Marie Kargman

When Eight Is Enough　104
Neal A. Kuyper

Insights into Establishing the Remarried
Household　107
Claire Berman

Buying a *New* Home for a *New* Family　109
Neal A. Kuyper

Dealing with Discipline　111
Elizabeth Einstein

Helping Remarried Families Deal with Weekend
Children　114
Joan Weiss

Attempting to Reconcile Conflicting Interests in a
Stepfamily　117
Robert S. Weiss

How to Deal with Sexual Feelings in the
Stepfamily　119
Claire Berman

8. What Are the Children Feeling? 121

    The Question of Children at the Wedding 121
    Neal A. Kuyper

    "Is It All Right to Love My Stepparent?" 123
    Joan Weiss

    Surnames Cause Confusion for Courts and
    Families 126
    Marie Kargman

    Helping Older Children Adjust in a Blended
    Family 130
    Neal A. Kuyper

    "Now You Have a New Brother and Sister!" 132
    Frederic F. Flach, M.D.

    Teenagers Speak Out about Stepfamily Living 134
    Jeanne Belovitch

    Lessons from the Simple Words of Children 137
    Donna Bilbrey

9. Custody, Visitation Rights, and Child Support 139

    The Issue of Custody 139
    Robert S. Weiss

    Don't Litigate—Mediate 141
    Marie Kargman

    The Rights of the Noncustodial Parent 144
    Peter Cyr

    On Being a Good Absentee Parent 147
    Peter Cyr

    Child Support: A Public *and* Private Problem 149
    Jeanne Belovitch

Making Shared Custody Work Well 151
Patricia L. Papernow

The Experiences of Parents Who Share Custody 155
Kathleen Walker

10. Closing the Gap between the Schools and
     Stepfamilies 161

     Remarriage and Schools: Support or Sabotage 161
     Elizabeth Einstein

     Noncustodial Parents: You Have Legal Rights with
     the Schools 163
     Jeanne Belovitch

11. Holiday Celebrations Begin New Traditions 165

     Wishing for a Kodak Christmas 165
     Robert S. Weiss

     The Challenge of Holiday Celebrations 167
     Elizabeth Einstein

12. When There Are Racial or Religious Differences 171

     The Challenges of Making It as an Interracial
     Stepfamily 171
     David A. Baptiste, Jr.

     The Remarried Family with Two Faiths 173
     Bernard Bloomstone

13. From the Roman Catholic Church 177

     Current Positions on Divorce and Remarriage 177
     James J. Young

     Readiness for Remarriage 180
     James J. Young

Growing Ecumenical Cooperation about
Remarriage 183
James J. Young

14. My Story 187

My Story: When My Stepchildren Disappeared 187
Christina Mathers

My Story: Where Is Justice? 189
Donna Lynn Deeb

My Story: My Role as a Natural Mother and Now
as a Stepmother 192
Mari Ellen Sabol

My Story: The "Odd Couple" Families 194
Barbara J. Bryce

Sources and Resources 197
Index 201
About the Contributors 205
About the Editor 209

Preface

Many of you who will read this book grew up in a time when mothers and fathers lived together and divorce was considered culturally blasphemous.

I remember that on the street where our family lived in Worcester, Massachusetts, there was a girl who lived with her mother, grandmother, and grandfather. Debbie never talked about her dad; I never asked about him. Of the some twenty-five families on the street, she was the only child whose parents were divorced. Debbie and I were seven years old then. I didn't meet up with another child of divorce until I went away to college.

Birth control, divorce, and remarriage were hot potatoes throughout the fifties . . . not readily addressed publicly, while the burden of not having these options sanctioned took their toll privately. The complaints I remember overhearing when my mother and other women in the neighborhood got together for midmorning coffee centered around the guilt they felt about exercising birth control, the one more pregnancy they could no longer endure, and the divorce they'd never get.

All these dilemmas have eased over the past thirty years. Today, I count twelve different family structures operating in the United States. You may come up with more. There is the traditional family, where Mom stays home and Dad goes to work; the Dad-stays-home-and-Mom-works family; the both-spouses-work family; the single-parent family; the remarried family; the homosexual family; the unwed-teenager-with-child family; the nonmarital family; the foster care family; the interreligious family; the interracial family; and the communal family. No matter which category they fit into, all families strive for similar goals: financial stability, cooperation, harmony, emotional support, trust, and unconditional love.

Why are all these types of families flourishing in the United States when, by contrast, Switzerland only recently passed a law ending men's rights to make all decisions for their families? The last word on the complexity of the American family is not in yet. We don't even have conclusive answers as to whether things are better or worse for individual members of nontraditional families. We do know, however, that the people who make up nontraditional families—adults and children—are pioneers in new ways of living. They are stretching themselves and their roles as well as society's laws and institutions.

This book is for the pioneers in remarried families. Remarriage is a social phenomenon that has crept up on us with little warning. Today, one out of two marriages is likely to end in divorce, and two-thirds of this divorced group will remarry. It has also been estimated that 57 percent of these remarriages will end in another divorce—a rate that is higher than that for first marriages.

Why such a high divorce rate? A fundamental reason is that most members of remarried families feel they have failed. In attempting to achieve success the second or third time around, many deny they are experiencing family and individual problems. They interpret their difficulties as signals of yet another approaching failure, when, in fact, the problems and heightened emotions experienced by adults and children are to be expected as a common occurrence in remarried life.

Until a remarried couple understand that their family is different from the first-marriage family—not better, not worse, but different—it remains in jeopardy. In a remarried family, a percentage of your income or your spouse's most likely goes to another family. There are weekend visits from stepchildren. There may be bitterness from the previous marriage to deal with. There are stepchildren to parent—sometimes, stepchildren you don't even like. A former spouse may be trying to disrupt and manipulate your new marriage. And on it goes—situations and continuous challenges that demand new skills, new perceptions, new ways of thinking, and new information.

This book will alert you to situations you may encounter as a remarried family; help to provide insight into and understanding of the emotions you and other family members may be experiencing; and attempt to help you develop new skills for meeting the challenges of creating a whole and contented new family.

Of the seventy articles published here, sixty-four were published originally in the *Remarriage* newsletter, with some minor changes and additions made for this book. All these articles are written by experts, most of them men and women who are nationally recognized for their knowledge in the areas of divorce, remarriage, stepparenting, and family law. Others are experts who come to these pages to share with you their experiences and feelings as they lived through specific situations in remarriage and stepparenting. I hope all these contributions help your new family find and create the enrichment that is possible when you remarry.

Editor's Acknowledgments

This book evolved from the newsletter *Remarriage,* which ceased being published in March 1986. As founder and editor of *Remarriage,* I am professionally grateful to its publishers, Thomas Rosse and Raymond Gambino, M.D., whose emotional and financial commitment to the issues of remarriage opened the way for the many fine contributions that now represent the collection in this book.

John L. Welch of Wolf, Greenfield, & Sacks, P.C., Boston, provided me with legal counsel at a moment's notice and when funds were not available. I am deeply grateful for his guidance, his generosity, and his kindness.

To my brother Louis, I owe many thanks for the long and informative conversations we shared about marriage in twentieth-century America, and for his support.

To the writers of the *Remarriage* newsletter whose work has been selected to appear in this book, I am most grateful. They contributed their expert information and guidance on the numerous issues that arise in remarried families with an empathy and understanding for which the newsletter became recognized and which is now available here to assist many more adults and children in remarried families.

1

A Look at Family Life, American Style

More Than One Kind of Normal Family

Lillian Messinger

That poor child comes from a broken family. I don't want you to play with her. She only has one parent, and now her mother has married someone else and Elsa has become a stepchild. No wonder she is a problem child.

Stigmas like these continue to plague children of divorce and remarriage, even though nearly 50 percent of American marriages end in divorce and 75 to 80 percent of divorced persons remarry. The prognostication is that half of all American children will be stepchildren at some point in their childhood by the end of the twentieth century. This growing population of postdivorce families can no longer be viewed as deviant. Even though children have lived through pain and loss as their intact family has been disrupted by their parents' divorce and remarriage, their family is not broken. Their family has the same members, the same mother and the same father. The family has been reorganized, not broken up. Ex-spouses are still parents to their children.

Society's view of remarriage lags behind the reality of this new culture of remarried families. They form a different kind of family system, where children live with one biological parent and one step-parent, or divide their family life between a maternal home and a paternal home. Yet we hold onto a traditional concept of the "nor-mal" family—the intact, Dick-and-Jane family with both parents and their biological children all living together. In our contemporary society, the idea of life in a normal family must be broadened to accept the reality of alternative family life-styles. Family life may be in a one-parent household or in a household with one biological parent and a stepparent—both are normal. We must establish a wider range of what constitutes normal family living.

The model we have learned for first marriages and family life does not apply to second marriages and their families. Beyond some of the complexities of adjusting to first marriages, remarriages have some additional unique aspects for which there are no guidelines. The ambiguity of step-relations is probably the most complex aspect of family life for stepfamilies.

Married life, the first time around, usually begins with a couple who, before they begin to add children to the family, have *couple* time to adjust to each other and to their marriage. The couple then learn their parenting roles as they raise their children from infancy and through the various developmental stages. They know what to expect and what is expected from them. The parents usually share affection and responsibility for their children. Family members have fairly well defined functions physically, emotionally, and econom-ically.

The family of remarriage is different in most of these respects. First of all, its functions and structures are different. The family now consists of one biological parent and a stepparent who lives together with the children, while one biological parent lives away from the family household. The latter may be a noncustodial parent whose children visit periodically and are stepsiblings to a new part-ner's children. We lack an adequate model to confer a sense of nor-mality on this unfamiliar family structure and relationship.

Remarriage and the family invite basic questions: What is a fam-ily? What connection is there between ex-spouses as their children's biological parents? What relationship is there between the divorced, same-sex, biological parent and the new remarried stepparent, both of whom have responsibility for the same children? They all have ties to the children of the previous marriage. The ex-spouses of the first marriage have permanent biological ties to their children, whereas the family of remarriage is a social, not a legal, structure, with social rather than legal functions. Society tends to expect that once a marriage has taken place, an instant family is born—with instant love. Family life is expected to conform to the traditional view of the first family. But this model does not fit. People who enter remarriage with such hopes and expectations usually experience confusion and disappointment in the face of unaccustomed feelings and experiences. Even if they know how to be excellent parents to their biological children, they may have trouble coping with their feelings as stepparents. They also have no way of knowing to what extent their feelings fall within the normal range of other stepparents' experiences.

The unrealistic myth of instant families and instant love can be devastating. Remarried partners come together after experiencing loss in their previous marriages. There is no couple time; instead, it is immediately family time. The couple do not share earlier memories of the developmental stages. They are unfamiliar with personal and family idiosyncrasies, traditions, behavior, and personalities. They are expected to live together as a family before they begin to feel like a family. Each member has difficulty adapting to life in the intimacy of family life with its varied membership. Stepparents can have intense problems accepting the children of a former marriage, and a former love. Children may have intense problems accepting that the new partner is taking the place of the nonresident biological parent. They also may live with the threat that, now that they have lost one parent from the home, the stepparent may take away their other parent as well. New partners frequently complain that they are afraid to commit their love to a stepchild who will never be their child. They may resent the fact that no matter how much effort they make to please the child, and no matter how much responsibility they take for the child, there seem to be no rewards, whereas children may respond warmly to nonresident parents who may have minimal responsibility for their welfare.

New stepparents may have difficulty coping with their feelings about ex-spouses. For example, Maureen was infuriated when she came into a marriage where her husband and his ex-wife had established an amicable arrangement for sharing responsibilities for their two children. The parenting arrangement did not suit her life-style. She was left out of arrangements that affected her marriage, her husband, and her family life.

Remarriage requires accommodating formerly established plans to present marriage plans. It also requires that both partners realistically face the fact that remarriage where there are children from the previous marriage requires preparation and anticipation of what will fit the new family life-style. The divorce does not terminate the former marriage ties. Divorce is only between the couple, not between parents and child, nor between parents and each of the extended families of the ex-spouses. As sociologist Paul Bohannen states, "My ex-wife will always be my son's mother and my ex-wife's mother will always be his grandmother."

Reflections of a Family Court Judge

Ernest Rotenberg

One really does have to walk in an Indian's moccasins for more than a few days to be able to speak for the Indians. Many people claim to be experts when they really do not have such credentials.

Only those who have endured or participated in the pain of a divorce can feel the anguish, turmoil, and bitterness that is often engendered. Every day for the past thirty-seven years I have observed the tragedy of domestic relations in the courtoom. For twenty-five of those years I served as an advocate for a husband or wife, and for the last twelve years as the first judge of the family court over which I still preside.

My daily observations over these years have enabled me to empathize with the husbands and wives whose marital battle has supposedly ended, only to be revived on yet another day over another issue. The following reflections are my own and are not necessarily the views of my colleagues on the bench, nor of the Massachusetts trial court of which I am a part.

For three anguished days they battled. The most intimate details of their life together lay strewn before me in chaos and disarray. The judgment was announced. The trial day completed. The case closed. As I walked down the inner stairs to the corridor leading to the outside, I heard muffled voices. Two figures huddled together near the exit in the darkened passageway came into focus, silhouetted against the rays of the fast-setting sun. Arms around each other as if clinging together for solace were my two protagonists of twenty minutes before. As I approached they looked at me, and I looked at them. I said, "Whatever happened upstairs can still be scrapped. If you feel the way I think you do, come see me tomorrow and we will make another beginning." They did.

That was the only time in my experience that a contested trial ended so happily. Usually I see sorrow, desperation, anxiety, anger, and occasionally relief or indifference. That's when I tell myself there ought to be a better way than to preside as the funeral director at the interment of a deceased marriage.

Over the past fifteen years our society has dramatically altered its patterns of marriage, family life, and divorce. Since our systems reflect societal behavior, it is appropriate to examine carefully the skyrocketing divorce rate and its devastating impact on the court system, the welfare system, the economy, and, most important, the victims of family separation, especially the children.

In the early 1970s, the governmental bodies designed to deal with the consequences of a previously docile issue (divorce) were hard pressed to adapt to the rapid social changes accompanying a soaring divorce rate. The system was crippled by a new and unexpected demand for services. The situation was exacerbated by budgetary limitations, lack of personnel, the absence of trained social service professionals on the staffs of the judiciary, and a limitation of space as well as equipment.

Efforts have been made to meet this challenge, however, and the system has adapted in a number of significant ways. One major change has been the establishment of comprehensive mediation services within the probate and family court department, supplemented by appropriate staff increases, computerization, modernization, and a general reorganization of the trial court. Another important change is the availability of no-fault divorce and the shortening of the period before divorce will take effect, from six months to ninety days. The wage assignment law and federal support enforcement assistance (including the Internal Revenue Intercept Program), as well as comprehensive support collection and enforcement programs in each division of the family court and in the district court division, are important examples of the progress the system has made in dealing with the problems spawned by a burgeoning divorce rate.

Divorce always results in the fragmentation of families, causing complex collateral issues. Most fractionalized families do not stay that way for long. The social acceptance of divorce and subsequent remarriage has raised new issues that require review, analysis, and ultimately further adaptation by our culture as we move toward the twenty-first century.

Divorced individuals who choose to remarry are a rapidly growing group and may represent as much as 75 to 80 percent of the divorced and widowed population. Conflict resulting from remarriage can be both painful and expensive. Maintaining the first family is obviously difficult when it is compounded by the emotional and financial responsibilities of beginning a new family. Moreover, the courts have traditionally maintained the posture that *first families take priority over second families*. There have been no developments suggesting otherwise or indicating that any radical change is on the horizon. Those frustrated people directly affected by this philosophy might well ask why.

One major explanation concerns the economic impact of the rising divorce rate on U.S. society. The effect on our system of public welfare is well documented. It is a fact of life that families without wage earners must seek relief through publicly supported aid—relief that must be generated by monetary funds. Through its various programs and joint agreements with most state governments, the federal government has mandated quick and equitable enforcement of child support and alimony orders made by the courts. Many new support enforcement programs are on the rise, and it is clear that the governmental bodies that once lagged behind the divorce rate have rapidly begun to catch up with the times. Judges as public trustees are mandated to reflect this posture, with little latitude. Hence the demand that a person must take care of his estranged family first continues to persist for lack of any other answers.

This is not to say that, as a representative of society, a judge cannot be compassionate, concerned, and innovative. As a trial judge I am not permitted to make new law, but I am required to put into effect existing pronouncements from our appellate courts. I have always felt that the Fourteenth Amendment should apply to the second spouse and the children of a second marriage. These innocent people are entitled to the equal protection of the law. They have a right to receive all the benefits that the Constitution of the United States can give them. The Fourteenth Amendment was passed shortly after the Civil War on July 28, 1868. Its first paragraph says:

> All persons born or naturalized in the United States and subject to the jurisdiction thereof, are citizens of the United States and of the State in which they reside. No State shall make or enforce any law which shall abridge the privileges and immunities of citizens of the United States; nor shall any State deprive any person of life, liberty, or property without due process of law; nor deny to any person within its jurisdiction the equal protection of the laws. . . .

I fully recognize that this concept flies in the face of case law in the Commonwealth of Massachusetts, which seems to hold that a person who remarries is presumed to have the wherewithal to support a new family financially. Such a pronouncement cannot always be true. Only time will tell in what way existing law will change, and how it will affect the life-styles of families of second marriages.

Second Families Go Unprotected by the Law
Donna Bilbrey

Lawmakers and courts have spent years writing and enacting legislation to protect the original family from the disaster of divorce. Their laws clearly provide the child of the first marriage with certain rights and financial support until adulthood.

In most states child support is awarded on the basis of the noncustodial parent's income. Its goal is to maintain the child's life-style as close to predivorce conditions as possible. The majority of child support payments are made by the father to the mother; the father is still awarded custody in only about 10 percent of cases.

In the court's hurry to protect children of divorce, however, it has left many children unprotected. Babies of second marriages are virtually on their own. According to Helen Garfield, professor of law at Indiana University, there are no laws on the books protecting the rights of second families. For our legal system today, second families simply do not exist.

The common view of most courts is that first obligations come first, a theory that seems to make sense until it is tested in the real world. How does a parent decide which child gets new shoes or receives medical treatment? By order of birth? The child of which marriage goes to college when there isn't enough money to send both? This particular dilemma clearly illustrates the lopsidedness of the law. The child of the first marriage can get a court order demanding that the father pay for college costs. The child from the second marriage, however, is entitled only to what is left over.

The second wife also suffers from lack of protection from the courts. Many second wives enter into their new marriages with jobs and incomes of their own, as well as their own children. Most second wives are fully aware of the financial obligations of their new husbands toward their former families and accept this as part of the arrangement. The wedding bells have barely begun to fade, however, when a *petition to modify* is at the door. The former wife would like an increase in support. The court grants the increase because it determines that the husband's living expenses have been reduced as a result of the second wife's income.

From this experience, the second wife learns that her income is no longer hers, but a mere extension of her husband's. And although the law does excuse her as a stepparent from any legal obligations to support her stepchildren, it is in fact awarding additional support based on her income.

The current trend toward remarriage in this country must also lead to acceptance of the second family. *Second* does not mean *second best*. The average age of the American child at the time of the parents' divorce is six years old. Parents of a child this young most likely will become parents again in the next marriage. We cannot continue to penalize children for not being born into the first marriage.

Many advocacy groups around the nation are recognizing the need for new laws to protect the second family. Some of them are Parents' and Children's Equality of Indiana; Ohio Fathers' Family Rights Association; Coalition Organized for Parental Equality of

Portland, Maine; American Child Alliance of Kansas City; and Texas Fathers for Equal Rights of Houston.

We need new legislation that reflects the present-day way of married life and protects all families equally and fairly under the law.

Stepfamilies in England, France, and the Netherlands
David A. Baptiste, Jr.

In the summer of 1985 I attended a clinical conference in the Netherlands and also visited England and France. In these countries I spoke informally with mental health professionals—psychologists, psychiatrists, counselors, and social workers—about issues affecting remarried families and stepfamilies. The general impressions I gained from these conversations include the following:

England, France, and the Netherlands do not perceive stepfamilies to be any more at risk than biological families who seek therapy.

The number of stepfamilies in these countries is relatively small compared to the number in the United States.

Stepfamilies in these countries do not appear to be experiencing any significant difficulties in adjusting to stepfamily living. They tend not to seek psychotherapy to as great an extent as American stepfamilies.

Stepfamilies appear to be more accepted as bona fide families in these countries than they are in the United States.

The following are some impressions of the situations of stepfamilies in these three countries:

England

The divorce rate is higher than it was ten years ago, but not as high as in the United States. England's divorced do not remarry as often or as quickly as Americans. The English tend to marry for the first time later in life than Americans do. They also live with their partners for longer periods of time before remarrying after divorce. For many, especially in the twenty- to thirty-five-year-old range, living together without benefit of marriage appears to be replacing remarriage after divorce.

Despite the tendency to cohabit rather than remarry, there are numerous stepfamilies in England, especially among the black West Indian population. As in the United States, most stepfamily problems come to therapy by way of the children's problems, which frequently extend to the adult couple. Because of the large numbers of ethnic minorities in England, many of the stepfamilies seeking therapy are interracial.

France

Despite its large Roman Catholic population, France's current divorce rate is reported as increasing, compared with ten years ago. Divorced French also tend to delay remarriage. Although there are many stepfamilies in France, the mental health professionals with whom I spoke did not have large numbers of stepfamilies in their case loads. Unlike their U.S. counterparts, most French stepfamilies who come to therapy are formed as a result of a spouse's death rather than divorce. Problems between the couple, rather than between stepparent and stepchild, appear to be the more frequent disturbance in remarried families.

The Netherlands

The divorce rate in the Netherlands is reported to be holding steady. Nonmarital cohabitation appears to be more prevalent among the Dutch than the English or French. Stepfamilies in the Netherlands do not seek therapy to as great an extent as the English and French, who in turn prefer it less than the Americans. Most of the problems the Dutch bring into therapy concern incompatibility between spouses, rather than between stepparents and stepchildren.

2

Is It Time to Remarry?

Successful Marriages Are Renewed Marriages
Frederic F. Flach, M.D.

All second marriages are not successful—but all successful marriages are second marriages. This doesn't mean that divorce and remarriage must become a way of life. Rather, it reflects a basic rule of human nature. Inevitably, everything falls apart, particularly in the face of change, and must be renewed. Whether the relationship between you and your spouse is disrupted and then put together again within the same marriage, or whether you are entering married life with a new partner, the process of renewal is nearly identical.

Any single marriage is really a series of marriages. You are a young couple, starting out. Then you have a child, and you become two parents. You have teenagers in the house, struggling to find their own identities. They remind you of yourselves when you were young, and they also call your attention to a few strands of gray hair and a touch of stiffness when you try to get up after sitting awhile in a deep chair. Suddenly, the children are gone, and you spend your evenings talking about what to do and where to live after you retire.

Every new phase of your marriage calls for a major reappraisal of your own identity and the nature of your relationship. This is not just an intellectual exercise. It is an experience loaded with feeling and conflict. It is usually accompanied by some degree of depression as a response to the loss of yourself as you were, but it is a necessary prelude to recommitment and renewal.

Obviously, many of us do not weather these episodes successfully. In some cases, the basic ingredients of a good marriage may not have been there to begin with. Today's loosening of social restrictions and expectations has made it easier for many of us, with or without good reason, to end marriages that are going through disruptive phases instead of staying with them until key issues are resolved and new strength in the relationship is discovered.

This cycle of disruption and reintegration can be considered a universal law of nature, which applies to practically every human endeavor. Ideally, we would like to master every such episode successfully, but being human, we are bound to make mistakes. All that nature demands, it seems to me, is that we learn from our mistakes, thus setting the stage for renewal.

The end of one marriage and the beginning of a new one can be viewed simply as another reflection of this same cycle. A second marriage is a form of rebirth. You will not escape the pain and challenges of the cycle there, any more than you could the first time. Ups and downs will be unavoidable. But you clearly will improve your prospects for success if you enter upon and live through your second marriage looking on it as an experience of reintegration. A second marriage is not the best of a bad bargain, a compromise, or an opportunity about which you should feel guilty because it may be built on ruins of your past. Rather, to repeat, a second marriage is an experience of reintegration.

Philosophy is a big word that tends to scare many of us away. Yet all it means is a point of view about things that helps us make sense of our lives. Considering a second marriage as a logical event in the reconstruction of your life—an integral part of the renewal process—can give you a philosophy that can only serve to increase your chances of making it work well.

The Advantages and Challenges
of Remarrying

Frederic F. Flach, M.D.

For those of you who have been divorced, there are some decided advantages to marrying again. In the first place, it may be good for your taxes. More important, you may live longer. Medical statistics suggest that married people live longer and have better general health than the unmarried. This is especially true for men; women generally appear to adjust much more successfully to living alone.

Why does remarriage strengthen your physical and mental resourcefulness? The answer isn't entirely clear, but we can make some intelligent guesses. There is substantial evidence that a significant social network—family members, friends and co-workers, with whom we have meaningful and lasting relationships—enables us to meet the challenges of life much more effectively than going it alone. Among patients who have suffered mental and emotional illnesses, for example, the rate and extent of recovery are very favorably influenced by the existence of such a network. Such support undoubtedly contributes to the maintenance of physical health as well. Many physicians believe that the fact that women have longer life spans than men can be explained by their readiness to create and sustain close, confiding, open relationships with others; men, on the other hand, tend to be private, obsessed with competitive concerns, afraid to admit their frailties, and living much of the time at arm's length from other men.

We know that most people have maternal and paternal instincts. In spite of the current constructive emphasis on finding oneself and developing a career direction before marriage, most young single people are searching for a satisfactory sexual and human relationship with someone that will endure in the context of marriage. This desire, which at times can become a preoccupation, is no less intense among the divorced.

The wish to remarry, however, is not always readily fulfilled. Even when the opportunity arises, the decision to marry and the choice of partner is not always made prudently. I have seen any number of patients who have married a second time only to find themselves immersed in another nightmare. Some have married rapidly, on the rebound—to soothe feelings of rejection, restore self-esteem, or quiet the anguish of powerful, unmet dependency needs—before they have had a chance to gain confidence in their ability to stand on their own two feet. Some unwittingly seek out or are sought out again by the type of person with whom marriage was a disaster in the first place. Others go to the opposite extreme by overvaluing a particular trait a former spouse lacked, only to discover a few months or years into a new marriage that in stressing one particular attribute, such as kindness or financial responsibility, they have overlooked other significant sources of incompatibility.

Making the right choice is only the first step in establishing a successful second marriage. There are a number of predictable challenges that must be mastered. You are fortunate if you have gained enough insight into yourself and the problems of your previous marital relationship not to repeat the same mistakes. Nor can you afford to carry with you into a new marriage the ghosts of your former one. Your new husband or wife will remind you in certain ways of your previous one. To varying degrees we all resemble each other, even though we possess our own individuality. Reminders of a former marriage can become focal points for conflict and dissatisfaction unless you remember that they are only fragments of a relationship. Your present relationship has a very different character when it is considered as a whole. You may even miss some of the better moments of your past marriage—and there are usually some. You must be careful not to expect a new spouse to be everything you ever hoped for.

These are some of the psychological struggles you can anticipate. There are some very pragmatic ones as well. How will you integrate two sets of children and in-laws into the context of your new marriage? What will you do about old friends? What will you do about old, favorite pieces of furniture, scrapbooks, photographs, albums, and other memorabilia? Most of all, what will you do about your sense of independence, carved out with blood and tears between marriages?

There are ways to cope successfully with every one of these stresses if you anticipate them and take the time to learn how. In the end, you will not only ensure a mentally and physically healthier life, but will discover a richer one as well.

Love Is Not All . . . Success in Remarriage Requires Much More
Paula Ripple Comin

Marriage is a basic right of every human being. The fact that Americans continue to be the most marrying people known in human history gives testimony to the validity and beauty of marriage as a way of life for most people.

High divorce rates have not significantly altered marriage rates. And the fact that more than 70 percent of divorcing persons remarry, half of them within the first twelve months after their divorce, is adequate witness to the desire for the friendship and companionship associated with marriage.

Many writers have discussed the cultural and personal causes of divorce in first marriages, but little has been written about the important question of why divorce rates are significantly higher in second marriages than in first marriages.

The basic friendship and communication skills that apply to first marriages are equally important in remarriage. In a society where people are commonly lovers first, it is sometimes difficult to discern whether or not they are also good friends.

Since human beings are not born with an automatic knowledge of how to be friends, development of good friendship skills begins at birth and continues throughout life. Such qualities as mutual respect for each other's gifts and limitations, the ability both to give and to receive love, the willingness to give and to seek forgiveness, the ability to deal with conflict, the capacity to listen even when it is difficult to do so, and the ability to speak affirming words are important and basic components of friendship in marriage. They also must be learned.

The fact that divorce rates for second marriages are higher (including rates for persons who have lost a spouse through death as well as divorce) is little known and surprising to some. The phrase *love is not all* can serve as a beginning for our reflections. It can lead us into some considerations of special areas that require attention from both partners in remarriage. These areas, though not totally absent from first marriages, do require added thought in remarriage.

1. *Past patterns of relating:* Santayana's statement that those who have not learned from the mistakes of the past are condemned to repeat them is borne out in the painful insights of men and women who have experienced more than one divorce. Human beings do not automatically change their behavior simply because they change partners. Destructive patterns in a first marriage will surely make their way into a second one unless some investment has been made in identifying and dealing with destructive behavior. One of the questions too many people who plan to remarry cannot answer is: *What have you learned about yourself since your divorce?*

2. *Respecting one another's past:* Each person who seeks to marry, whether divorced or not, marries a personal history, including hurts and areas of intense sensitivity. Caring for each other does not mean ignoring these areas or expecting them to disappear with the advent of a new love. What is required is gentle caring and a willingness to listen to feelings and even irrational responses sometimes triggered by associations that have nothing to do with the present relationship. A person who has never been married also carries into the relationship a past that requires both attention and respect.

3. *Realistic expectations of oneself and the other:* The fact that we may have learned some things about ourselves through the difficult process of either death or divorce and the desire to love a new person well does not mean we will never again fail either ourselves or others. Accepting our humanness means understanding that we will always love imperfectly—we have no other way. The fact that we are now a few years older and have added experiences does not necessarily mean we are proportionately wiser, nor does it insure us against errors in judgment.

4. *Some hurts are only finally healed in a new relationship:* People experienced in working with those going through a divorce believe that the period of recovery may be as long as three to five years. Even highly motivated people who have found good support systems and have taken time to deal with the loss of a relationship need to know that a portion of the healing can only happen as they seek to relate to a new person in a different way. Behavior and ways of relating do not change in isolation; neither can it all be done in groups.

5. *Space for the former spouse:* Dealing both practically and emo-

tionally with one's former spouse does not end with the choice of a new partner. Finances, children, and in-laws may necessitate some kind of ongoing relationship with the former spouse. Neither the courtroom pronouncement nor the funeral is a final step.

6. *The children of a former marriage:* One certain piece of information about the children of divorce (or those who have lost a parent to death) is that they do as well as their parent or parents do. The more parents invest in dealing constructively with their own lives, the easier the adjustment for their children. And since children generally remain attached to both parents, avoiding criticism of the other spouse in the presence of the children is a wise decision in fostering the continued growth of one's own relationship with them.

7. *The quest for a new community of friends:* The loss of a former community of friends is a common experience of those who have lost a spouse to death or divorce. Discovering new friends together thus becomes a project that is as important as it is sometimes difficult. Good friends provide important support to new marriage relationships. A two-person world can all too quickly become a very small world, in need of outside light and life.

8. *Making time for play:* Good people who take their lives seriously are often highly motivated to work hard at those things that are important to the marriage. Such an overserious environment can do harm to a relationship. Making time to laugh and play together deserves a high priority.

These are just a few of the important considerations in remarriage. All the love and good will in the world will not prevent or remove the need to remember that Dostoevsky's assessment of the situation is accurate: *Love in dreams is easy. Real love is a sometimes harsh and demanding reality.*

From "Never Again" to "I Do"
Elizabeth Einstein

After grueling first experiences with marriage, newly single people often say, "I'll never marry again." But in fact within three to five years almost everyone who wants to tie another marital knot will do so.

Who remarries and why? How does "never again" become "I do"? According to Census Bureau reports, among those forty-five years old or younger, more than 80 percent of divorced men and 75 percent of divorced women remarry. Parents remarry sooner than people without children, perhaps because they need help in child rearing or finances. People with lower incomes marry sooner, also most likely from need. Those who are in poor health and those who are older have a harder time finding a mate and may have to wait longer. But when the desire to remarry is powerful, and people are motivated to find another partner, they do. Unfortunately, some of the reasons people remarry are not wise ones.

People remarry—or marry for the first time—to meet their own needs. Some needs are "good" ones, and it is healthy to seek their fulfillment in marriage. But other needs may be rooted in dependency or unresolved personal issues. Usually, when people marry or remarry for wrong reasons, they eventually become unhappy. The high divorce rate among remarrieds seems to indicate that too many people are saying "I do" for the wrong reasons. This is especially traumatic when children are involved and they experience another family breakup.

For some people, remarriage provides an escape from society's pressures. Few social support systems operate for the divorced, especially for single women with children. Some adults feel guilty if their children lack a second parental figure who is in the house full time. Others feel overwhelmed by the challenge of single parenthood. Many cannot make ends meet financially and allow economic pressures to blur emotions. The feeling labeled *love* may be colored by an unconscious fear of not being able to make it on one's own.

Rebound remarriages occur for at least two reasons. If there is hostility between divorcing partners, one may remarry quickly for revenge or to soothe a wounded ego. Or hasty remarriage can result from an affair begun during the former marriage. A tryst that may have served as a happy and exciting escape during the painful period of a marriage's disintegration may not have the long-term *stuff* of which a strong marriage is made. Some people marry their transition person: that special human being who has helped them through the loneliness and hard times. When such a relationship is based on a caring friendship, it may work. Too often, however, it reflects romance and sexual adventure rather than more important and lasting qualities.

When people remarry for some of these *wrong* reasons, the sweet future they envision tends to sour quickly. The relationship lacks the basic glue to hold a marriage together.

As people prepare for remarriage, they may or may not be aware of its predictable stages. Getting through the loss of a mate is painful. For a time, all one can do is endure the guilt, anger, and ambivalent feelings that are part of this process. But as people heal, forgive, and let go, they can pick up the necessary building blocks and begin to take stock of themselves. Along the way, many make important connections and discoveries that will make a difference in the direction of their lives.

Men struggle with their feelings and with learning about domestic duties. For most women, the challenge is to earn enough money and build a sense of identity apart from their former role of wife. The divorce-and-remarriage journey is difficult, but most men and women experience personal growth as they cope and begin to meet new people. New relationships and interests help formerly marrieds discover new facets of themselves and what they really want from life. Many people enter therapy and learn about their darker sides, which sheds light on their share of responsibility for the former marriage's end. As self-esteem and self-confidence rise, these positive qualities become an antenna that attracts new people. Such experiences provide a frame of reference within which people ultimately choose new mates.

As time passes and the challenges of transition are mastered, people become able to trust themselves and their choices. They begin to consider once again sharing life with one special other. Even adults, enjoying the rewarding single lives they've created from their loss—enough money, successful careers, fine relationships with friends and family—ultimately find that the *missing piece* is a person with whom to share their life and love. These people remarry for *good reasons:* the need for intimacy, companionship, and access to a sexual partner.

At this point, many people meet a new partner. It may begin as a friendship with a colleague at work or in the community theater that eventually leads to a commitment to remarriage. This point of commitment is an important time for last-minute wondering: Do I really know enough about myself to make it work this time? Do I know what I want in a mate? Have I resolved some of my own issues that intruded on the former marriage?

Research shows that people in happy remarriages are just as happy as those in first marriages. But even then, once the romantic fireworks cool down, remarriage is hard work, especially when it creates a stepfamily. Those who take the time to work themselves through the lengthy divorce process and to become independent people improve their chances of choosing good mates. Independence makes *choice* possible. A remarriage between two mature, independent people—who *choose* to be together—contains the basic glue needed to keep a marriage together. Getting information about remarriage and stepfamily living as well as giving yourself and other family members time to adjust provide even a greater edge for success.

When positive factors provide the foundation for remarriage, success can be very sweet.

Are You Ready to Remarry?

Elizabeth Einstein

A loving and successful remarriage depends on how well adults prepare themselves and their children. The *getting-ready* time of courtship is different from the first time around. Important connections that will make a difference for you during remarriage include four basic tasks: resolving, rebuilding, relinking, and remarrying. By responding as honestly as you can to these questions, you can check how you're doing in each of these stages.

Stage I: Resolving

Dealing with former relationships is crucial to forming healthy new ones. The first important task is to work through some difficult feelings about the ending of your marriage so you can work toward achieving an *emotional divorce*. Have you:

Tried to work through differences in counseling?

Worked with a divorce mediator to settle economic and child-rearing issues in a cooperative way?

Developed a workable form of shared parenthood with your former spouse?

Confronted your feelings rather than denying them?

Gained support from friends and family?

Allowed forgiveness—of yourself and your former mate?

Stage II: Rebuilding

Taking the time to rebuild yourself into a strong, independent human being will provide the basis for your share of a solid couple relationship. Because the skills and strength of the married couple are the cornerstone of a stepfamily's stability, it is important to see how you are doing. Have you:

Developed a support network of friends and family?

Gained new skills around the house?

Started working or school?

Learned to manage money and support the family?

Built a social life and begun dating?

Restored trust in self and others?

Forgiven yourself for the sense of failure you harbor?

Stage III: Relinking

One you have committed yourself to a new relationship, many tasks need to be confronted, especially if the remarriage creates a stepfamily. Addressing and discussing as many of the following issues as possible can give you a head start on building a strong stepfamily. Have you:

Begun to discuss remarriage with your children?

Discussed child-rearing methods with your future mate?

Introduced your children to your future spouse and spent time together?

Identified individual parenting styles?

Worked with a counselor on trouble spots?

Read some information about stepfamily living?

Decided where to live?

Clarified the issue of adding an "our" child?

Assured the children that their biological parents will not be replaced?

Stage IV: Remarrying

Celebrating with your children in a creative ceremony can pave the way for a joyous beginning to your remarriage. Taking on the role of stepparent requires all the advantages you can muster. Ask yourself these final questions. Have you:

Discussed the challenges that lie ahead with your children?

Sought your children's feelings and listened to their concerns?

Allowed your children to express negative as well as positive feelings?

Celebrated with the children and included their ideas in the ceremony?

Planned family meetings to set up rules and routines, and to clarify responsibilities?

Kept your expectations realistic?

A successful remarriage begins as your former marriage ended. The time in between can be the most important investment you ever make. *Resolving* your relationship with a former spouse leaves you free to begin a new one, without the past impinging on the future in destructive ways. *Rebuilding* yourself as a strong person provides the base you need for the challenging role of stepparent. *Relinking* with a new mate in a positive way requires looking ahead at some major hurdles and planning wisely. *Remarrying* the new person you have come to trust and love provides the potential for a successful remarriage.

Congratulations!

3

The Cold Facts about Remarriage: Money, Prenuptial Agreements, and Wills

Dare We Talk about Money?

Claire Berman

"Half of George's income goes toward alimony and child support," says Sue, George's second wife. "It isn't easy for him to meet those obligations. Yet when his daughter Alison arrives for a visit, she's always dressed in outgrown, outworn jeans. With all the money George's ex-wife gets, she certainly ought to be able to buy the child some decent clothes. I'm ashamed to go anywhere with her."

"Barbara's 'ex' is constantly behind in his child support payments," says Don, Barbara's present husband. "I have had to assume the major support of my stepchildren. I can accept that. But what galls me is that whenever I say 'no' to my stepson about something I think he doesn't need (like his own stereo) or that we can't afford (like his own stereo), the boy's response is, 'My father will buy it for me.' And he's generally right."

Money creates stresses in most families—there never seems to be enough to meet everyone's needs *or* desires. Not surprisingly, it causes even more anxiety for remarried families, whose financial affairs tend to be far more complex and emotionally burdened.

To begin with, a husband and wife in a second family are more likely than a first-wed couple to have individual property—a home, some savings, part of a divorce settlement. And they are less likely to feel comfortable about placing all their assets into a common account. Having had one marriage fail, both husband and wife may want to keep money aside—just in case there's another divorce. They are wary of making a total commitment—financially or emotionally. They hold back.

In addition, the remarried family may not be a financially independent unit. Like George in our first example, many divorced men have obligations to their first family. And like Sue, many second wives resent the fact that money must go out of the remarriage household.

Then there are those families that rely on money coming in—generally in the form of support payments from the noncustodial parent. But suppose, as Don discovered in our second example, those payments cannot be relied on to arrive in a timely fashion (or, in some cases, at all). The new husband finds that he's expected to assume greater financial responsibility for his stepchildren.

It's no wonder resentments build. What *is* surprising, in the light of all this, is the reluctance of remarried couples to talk about money either before or after remarriage. Instead, Sue focuses on torn jeans and Don complains about the *sugar daddy behavior* of his wife's former husband.

Men and women entering a remarriage must take a realistic look at money—not only how much there is and how it is to be allocated, but at how each of them *feels* about money. Will the second wife resent the regular expenditures that are required to support the children of a previous marriage? (Note: They have *not* become "previous" children.) If support payments *into* the newly formed household are not forthcoming, will the second husband take on the responsibility? With reasonably good grace? Will the current financial responsibilities preclude the new pair from having a child? Is this important? To both partners?

Once couples have been honest about money, they can move on to create what I refer to as an *emotionally realistic budget*—one that takes into account both dollars *and* sense.

For example: Once Sue dared to be candid, she admitted that she resented feeling deprived because of the financial burden caused by George's sizable monthly child support payments. She and George talked this over and decided that Sue would withhold a set sum from her own weekly paycheck, which she could use for anything she wanted. Last year Sue treated herself to a week's holiday at a spa. With her own needs taken care of, Sue is less jealous of how George spends his money. Although this solution may not work for every couple in a similar situation, what is important is that this is an *emotionally realistic budget* for George and Sue.

A second case in point: When Marty met Pam, he was living apart from his wife and four children. Pam, a divorcee, and *her* three children lived in a house that she supported. In time Marty obtained a divorce, married Pam, and moved into her home. Because of his large financial responsibility (to four children), he is unable to contribute much to the running of his present home. In essence, he pays room and board, increasing his contribution during those weeks when his own children visit (and he knows the grocery bills will be greater).

That is fine with Pam. "I knew Marty had four children to support," she says. "I couldn't respect him if he didn't continue to meet his obligations to them." Marty and Pam's arrangement might not satisfy other couples. No matter. What's important here—and I cannot stress this too strongly—is that they have mutually arrived at a way of dealing with money that incorporates the reality of *both* their *financial* situation *and* their *emotional* needs. It works *for them*.

In one study, couples were asked to give the reasons for the failure of their *second* marriages. The two answers most frequently given were *money* and *children*, in that order. Do couples dare to talk about money? That they dare *not* to do so is becoming increasingly clear.

Is a Prenuptial Contract Necessary?

Neal A. Kuyper

Although a prenuptial contract is usually not necessary in a first marriage because there is little collective baggage (a few articles of furniture, an older car, some recreational equipment, and eager anticipation of the future generally constitute the entire estate), a second marriage in midlife often brings with it a bevy of children, a brace of homes, assorted investments, myriad items of personal property, and a justifiable concern for protecting one's own assets. Although some people believe the sacrament of marriage itself implies that all resources are automatically merged, others feel it's only logical to place some or all of their assets in separate estates.

Resistance to such an open disclosure of property, debts, and investments may be due to differences in resources. But more often it's because such openness is new; *what's yours/what's mine* was simply not a factor when today's middle-aged bride and groom were married previously. And one or both of the parties may feel a prenuptial agreement indicates ambivalence toward the new marriage.

A review of property and assets can help important areas surface that would otherwise seem of little consequence. In discussing and preparing material for the prenuptial contract, a couple may well learn additional, helpful information about each other's values, attitudes toward property, and life-styles.

Love and caring remain the most crucial binding force in any new marriage. But love can run dry and caring turn to hostility, unless the financial structure of the relationship is understood, agreed on, and clearly stated in a legal document that puts a couple's house in order *before* the fact. The following are some items to consider as you start planning your own prenuptial agreement:

1. *Real estate:* List all separate real estate holdings with their values, indebtedness, and payments. Will these remain separate property or go into joint tenancy? Will you sell your home(s)? Invest in a common domicile?

2. *Assets:* List all stocks, bonds, money market funds, annuities,

savings accounts, second mortgages, and money owed to you. What portion will be merged and what will remain separate property?

3. *Furniture and furnishings:* Again, what will be jointly and what separately owned? Will some items be sold or given away?

4. *Pension funds:* Determine if anyone else (such as a former spouse) has a claim on your pensions. Will that change with the remarriage? Will the beneficiary designation change?

5. *Insurance:* Decide who the beneficiary will be after the marriage takes place. The amount may have to be reevaluated, and additional coverage for the spouse and any minor children considered.

6. *Debts:* List all payments (other than those covered in item 1) that will remain at the time of your wedding.

7. *Promises:* Don't forget any assurances, both oral and written, that may have been made to the children concerning education, weddings, business ventures, health insurance, support, and the like.

8. *Checking accounts:* Separate or joint with survivorship? Household account—who pays into it, and how much? Safe deposit box—joint or separate? Keys—private domain?

9. *Former spouse:* If the previous marriage ended in divorce, all obligations, financial and otherwise, to the former spouse should be disclosed, including child support payments. If the former spouse died, detail any provision of his or her will that will change your financial structure once you remarry.

10. *Credit cards:* List all. Will they remain separate or become joint? What liberty should you give each other?

11. *Automobile:* Separate or joint ownership? How will the insurance be paid?

12. *Employment:* Will earnings be kept separate or joined? Does the marriage make it inconvenient for either party to continue working? What effect will future retirement have?

13. *Parents:* Does either party have aging parents who are dependent now or may become so? Will they live with you? What financial help will be given?

14. *Children:* What are each party's financial and/or parental responsibilities? If a child has special needs, what are they and how will they be handled?

15. *Religious practices:* Same church? Separate with no interference? Contributions—from which fund?

16. *Personal needs:* Itemize personal habits, allergies, climate or

geographical preferences, major aversions. How will you accommodate each other?

17. *Wills:* Specify that separate wills will be executed; itemize provisions each person should make for the other in his or her will.

18. *Periodic revisions:* Formally agree to review the prenuptial agreement in three years and, if modifications are in order, to seek counsel of an estate planner or attorney.

For those who are not convinced that a prenuptial contract is the way to go, let's look at three case histories:

Margaret had no prenuptial agreement before her second marriage to a prospering dentist, although she brought to the marriage a $125,000 inheritance. Her new husband's life-style required a lot of money for his five children and his expensive cars. He proceeded to invest Margaret's money in a tax shelter scheme for one of his sons—a guitar factory that later went bankrupt. The marriage was dissolved, and Margaret spent $25,000 in an unsuccessful attempt to reclaim her own money. A prenuptial agreement would have protected Margaret's inheritance from becoming commingled with community property.

Ted and Sally had been married only four months when, one evening, Sally nonchalantly announced, "Oh, by the way, we have to repay Mother the $8,000 I owe her." Ted was horrified: What else was his new bride holding back? A prenuptial agreement would have put all the cards—Sally's *and* Ted's—right out on the table.

Linda and Merle had been married a year when he developed cancer. Before the marriage, he had placed all his insurance and money market funds in a joint account with his parents; he had also given them a lien on his house to protect it from his ex-wife. When Merle died six weeks after his illness was diagnosed, he left almost nothing for his wife, their child, or his three children by his previous marriage. His parents are still claiming the money belongs to them. A prenuptial agreement and a change of beneficiaries would have prevented this tragedy.

A Look at Antenuptial Agreements

Doris Jonas Freed

The current revolution in family law has manifested itself in a number of ways, one of which is the expression of public policy with regard to antenuptial agreements. The move from the idea of marriages as a *status* to the idea that it is a *contract* has rapidly accelerated, and the coverage permitted by antenuptial agreements has increased. Today, in practically all states, an antenuptial agreement is acceptable and enforceable in court where inheritance rights are waived.

Crowded matrimonial calendars in practically all states, together with the great incidence of divorce, have combined to effect these results and to make it sensible that the parties, at least to some degree, be permitted to write their own ticket. The antenuptial agreement today, for the most part, is not merely a concession to senior citizens to permit them to leave the bulk of their estates to children of a former marriage. Even second marriages between young people may be terminated by divorce, not death.

The National Conference of Commissioners on Uniform State Laws has completed a model act (the Uniform Antenuptial Agreement Act) that has been approved by the American Bar Association and has been adopted by the states of Virginia and California.

The former notion that antenuptial agreements are inconsistent with the status of marriage is being steadily eroded, and statutes have greatly expanded freedom of contract in this area. Yet differences exist from jurisdiction to jurisdiction, and antenuptial agreements are not usually given automatic enforcement.

For example, in California, Colorado, Illinois, Indiana, Iowa, Kentucky, Minnesota, Ohio, Oklahoma, Oregon, and Washington, antenuptial agreements have been limited to property rights only. Any waiver of support rights has been held to be against public policy and hence void. A number of states insist on full disclosure of the extent of property rights waived. In some, disproportionality between the parties' assets leads to a presumption of concealment of the true extent of the property waived, and in several, lack of opportunity to seek independent legal advice has sufficed to overturn antenuptial contracts.

Fairness and the absence of fraud, duress, and overreaching are routinely considered predicates to enforcement in most states, whereas Massachusetts and Ohio specify that antenuptial agreements be fair and reasonable.

Negotiations preceding antenuptial agreements are more difficult than those for separation agreements. With separation agreements, the marriage is known to be dead; all that remains is to divide the assets. With antenuptial agreements, however, negotiations can be very sticky since the marriage hasn't taken place yet and many prospective marriages never occur. More sensitivity is required of the attorney. Lack of independent counsel is not necessarily fatal as long as the agreement is based on full disclosure, the parties are fully informed of the significance of all waivers, there is no overreaching, and the provisions of the agreement are fair and reasonable. Likewise, the agreement must be free from fraud and duress. If an agreement meets these tests, it will be enforced normally even though a bad bargain may have been struck.

I recommend that all premarital agreements provide for four considerations: (1) the death of either party, (2) the division of property in the event of death, (3) spousal maintenance, and (4) disposition of the family residence. Stay away from custody and child support, which are subject to change by the court.

Remarriage and Writing a Will
Neal A. Kuyper

"When are we going to get the will written?" yells an irritated Judy, now in her seventh year of a remarriage with Keith.

"I'm not dying, so what's the big push?" Keith responds, equally disgusted by this weekly request of Judy's. "You and the kids will get all the money, so why worry?" Keith also knows that the real reason they have not written a will is their disagreement over its contents. It's complicated—Keith has three children from a former marriage and two from his present marriage. He feels a lot of guilt about leaving those three children at the time of his divorce. Now he wants to compensate for some of that pain by providing well for them in his will.

Judy is afraid she could be left with two small children and not enough funds, while a goodly portion of Keith's share of the estate goes to his three mature children. Judy feels two of Keith's other children have had their fair share during the past years because she and Keith made sacrifices for their education. Even though one of the children lives with her mother, Judy has agreed to help her finish high school and college with special provisions. When Keith says he wants his share of the estate divided equally among the five children, it angers Judy, who knows it puts her two preschool children at a disadvantage. After all, Keith's children have been draining Keith and Judy's finances for the last seven years.

Why do we all procrastinate when it comes to writing a will? Do we, like Keith, fear conflict? We all know it must be done, but we wait until our spouse applies the pressure. It is not a matter of cost, but simply of pulling the contents together and reaching some agreement. Judy wants the area of disagreement solved to protect herself and her two children in case Keith dies prematurely. The age of the children limits the amount of work she can do outside the home, and the mortgage payments alone would be overwhelming on a limited income. Even though she knows Keith is a loving husband who provides well for her, the very idea of his children from the former marriage receiving the same amount of money as their two preschoolers seems unfair.

A will is a written legal document that controls the disposition of property at the time of death. As part of the estate of the husband or wife, it designates who will receive property and other assets, and in what proportion. It is the *proportions* that concern Judy.

Judy would like Keith to will all of his estate to her; she would do the same in her will, leaving everything to him. Then each could provide for the smaller children. Judy would accept money being designated for the daughter living with his former spouse, but she especially needs to know that the home will be hers and that Keith has an insurance policy that would pay the remaining mortgage at the time of his death.

In case of a common death, as in an auto accident, Keith would like all his children to share and share alike in their estates. Again, one can understand why this ruffles Judy's feathers, since she is protecting those two younger children. Keith and Judy do agree that Judy's sister would be the appointed guardian if both of them died.

Al and Dorothy do not face the problem of minor children since all of their six children (four of his and two of hers) are now adults who have left the nest. Al has willed everything to his wife, and she to him. In case of a common death, 25 percent of their estate will go to three church-related organizations, and the rest to the six children, share and share alike. Since his four children received many of his things like silverware and china at the time of his remarriage (his first wife is deceased), Dorothy has now designated special items like her piano and silverware to her daughter. Al is in total agreement.

Since many items are not covered in the will, Al and Dorothy have drawn up a list of their desires on a sheet of paper. Al wants his books to go to his son and the word processor to a daughter. He has some World War II souvenirs that he wishes his grandson to have. Dorothy wants her jewelry left to her daughter, since it was a gift from her own mother. They both have indicated the type of memorial service they wish and the proper disposal of their remains. Although they feared an onslaught of depression would accompany their list making, instead, they were relieved as they placed their list in a safe deposit box at the bank.

How can you get the will written? *First*, sit down and each write out your wishes for the will. Then compare your lists to find areas of agreement and disagreement. If you cannot compromise, then get help from a friend, counselor, pastor, or attorney.

Second, call an attorney. You can ask the attorney the cost and what information is needed to draw up the will. The attorney may ask you to send your wishes in the mail. One office call may be all that is necessary to review the will and sign it. Some people attempt to do their own will, but I believe it is safer to have an attorney put it in legal form so that it will be in accordance with the laws of your state of residence.

Third, of course, put the will in a safe place. Some leave it in the attorney's office, others in a bank's safe deposit box. One family member should be told where the will is located. Al and Dorothy appointed the oldest son as executor; his signature gives him access to the safe deposit box. He also knows where to find the key if necessary.

Tips for Preparing a Will

1. If you have a prenuptial agreement, your wills should agree with that document. For example, the prenuptial agreement may

have made provision for a minor child who is now an adult. You may have set up separate estates and now, after years of marriage, commingled them. If some of the assets remain as separate estates, this must be noted.

2. If there are minor children, provision should be made for a guardian. Both wills need to be in agreement on this decision. You may want to make special financial provisions for minor children.

3. Is each spouse designating that all property and assets go to the other upon death? Are provisions for the children of the former marriage spelled out clearly?

4. Is a trust being considered for all the children or for a child who has special needs and requires a guardian for the trust fund?

5. Is there provision for prized possessions like books, record albums, jewelry, furniture? A friend of mine collects Indian artifacts and has willed them to a university. Do you have some jewelry from your grandmother that you especially want your grand-daughter to have?

6. If you are updating an old will, does it include changes in births, deaths, or the executor of the will?

7. Does either of you want to make a special bequest to a church, a school, a charity, or someone you want to remember?

8. Are the insurance policies' beneficiaries the same as in the will? For example, a man willed everything to his spouse but forgot that his insurance policies still had his mother as beneficiary. He had placed her name on the policies at the time of his divorce and not changed them after his remarriage.

9. Do the survivors' benefits on bank accounts also agree with the will? If not, is the reason for this difference noted in the will?

10. Have you given some consideration to probate and taxation costs to minimize these costs to the survivor at the time of death?

Many attorneys will have checklists as well. However, their list may not include some of the unique needs related to your remarriage.

Couples who have their legal house in order with a will find it reassuring. When the will was completed, Judy said, "Now I feel more secure if Keith should die. I want us to live to a ripe old age together. When I look at the ages of the children, this completed will lets me sleep with more peace."

Writing a will is not evidence of a morbid preoccupation with death but, rather, a way of making provisions for your spouse and children. It is an act of kindness. It also means you have made mature judgments about the distribution of your property and have provided for the care of your spouse and family. If you do not have a will, then the state has a process for distribution of your assets. How much better to have it be your decision. When it is all finished, you will breathe a sigh of relief and say, "It wasn't that bad after all—I'm glad it is finished."

4

Are You Prepared to Be a Second Wife?

Being a Second Wife

Donna Bilbrey

In the last five years, millions of women have found themselves in the role of second wife. Studies show that 60 percent of these women were unprepared for day-to-day married life with a man who had been married before.

What most second wives expect from their marriage is much the same as what first wives expect. Second wives, however, soon learn that their role in their new marriage is extremely complex. The intricate maze the second wife travels to find her place in her new family can be painful and filled with perplexing daily problems. Often she will have no clear idea of what is expected from her, and often she will anticipate too much.

One of the most difficult roles a new second wife faces is instant stepmotherhood. For the nearly two-thirds of women who were never married and were childless before marrying a previously married man, stepmothering presents an enormous adjustment. Depending on custody arrangements, a husband may expect his new wife to step into the role of full-time mother immediately, without the benefit of the nine months the natural mother had to prepare for the task. Without understanding and support from her new husband, a second wife may end up feeling like a substitute mother without experiencing the joy of feeling like a wife and a lover.

There are several ways a husband can ease his new wife's transition into the family. First, recall the phrase in the marriage vows, *forsaking all others*. In a first marriage these words are taken for granted: of course the husband will renounce all others. For the second wife, however, these words, at first glance, don't seem to fit—there's a former wife in the picture.

Yet in a second marriage it is especially significant for a husband to acknowledge *forsaking all others*. Many men carry an excess of guilt after the demise of their former marriage. They may feel guilty about not being with their children, about money, even about not being with their former wives. Guilt is *one* reason that divorcing men agree to alimony and child support payments far beyond their means. Because it is difficult for men to admit their feelings of guilt, these feelings often are carried into second marriages.

Guilt can and does destroy second marriages. The new husband should keep his obligations to his first family in perspective and realize that his future is with his present wife. It is the husband's job to make his new bride feel secure in her position.

Another way a husband can help his second wife is to discuss openly specific details of their daily living with respect to his children. Is she to cook all their meals, make their beds, do their laundry? Will discipline be a shared responsibility? The second wife can easily feel an outsider if she is not involved actively in the parental role. It is also vital to project a united front in matters involving children. Disagreements are better discussed in private.

What the second wife's role should *not* include is dealing with her husband's former wife as a go-between.

A second wife's role will never be crystal clear. She will be wise to expect certain amounts of confusion and conflict and not to drain herself emotionally trying to fit her idea of the "second wife" into a tidy package.

Although this role is filled with vague questions and undefined boundaries, one aspect of it is quite clear: your relationship as friend and lover to your husband. Romance should never be taken for granted or replaced with grocery shopping, laundry, and child care.

When you add humor, love, and laughter to the many roles of the second wife, you'll experience a universe of living most first wives never know.

A Second Wife, a Former Wife, and the Common Denominator

Marie Kargman

Rivalry among children for the time, attention, love, and money of their parents, commonly known as *sibling rivalry,* is familiar to all of us. Sibling rivalry, however, is but one form of kinship rivalry.

The remarried family also has its own special kind of kinship competitions. When the second wife and the former wife vie for the dollar and the attention of the shared former husband/present husband in the blended or remarried family, we have *former-wife rivalry.*

In a letter to "A Confidential Talk" in the November 1984 issue of *Remarriage,* a second wife describes in great detail all the obstacles she sees to the success of her second marriage, among them the $370 plus $90 for insurance per month that her husband gives his former wife out of his $25,000 annual income. In addition, the former wife sometimes asks for and receives additional sums of $50 to $100 a month for emergencies, plus help with clothes. "Now, how can I budget for our financial needs?" asks this second wife. Yet in another part of the letter she says, "My husband says we don't need a budget and what he gives his ex-wife and children is none of my business." (*Her* new husband expects her to carry her own financial weight in the marriage.)

This second wife is working full time. The former wife is going to school full time. The second wife goes to school, too, but takes only one course per semester. When she told her husband she would like to take more courses, he said he would have no part of it.

It is obvious from this letter that there has been no attempt to acknowledge emotionally that these two families share a common denominator, the husband. On the other hand, the second wife says that her former husband has remarried and that they and his new wife are on good terms: "I receive $100 a month from my ex and that is all."

Why is this second wife writing to "A Confidential Talk"? The answer lies in her own words: "I guess the bottom line is I do not have any criteria on which to judge the legitimate requests of an ex-wife, and the reasonable meeting of those needs." The letter is signed *Looking for enlightenment.*

What can we contribute to the enlightenment of this second wife who feels her husband "has not let go of guilt and attachment to their [his first family's] needs." From the tone of the letter, one can infer that this wife has conveyed to her husband her analysis of his guilt, along with her conviction that she is right.

I wonder how many husbands enjoy hearing a psychological analysis of their behavior from their wives? Wives were not meant to be their husbands' therapists. The right motive—wanting to help—cannot forestall the emotional response that must be expected: "Don't tell me what to do or why I do it! Stay out of my business."

This second wife's husband has been married to her for eight months. With his first wife he has two children, ages fourteen and eighteen, and he has been divorced for six years. It will take more time for him to detach himself enough from his first family to make the commitment his second wife is asking of their marriage.

Is this second wife asking the right question? How will "having criteria on which to judge the legitimate requests of an ex-wife" help this woman? Even if such criteria did exist, confronting her husband with them won't improve their relationship. It will only highlight her competitive behavior, perhaps forcing her husband to defend his former wife even more.

What should this second wife do? She is going to counseling, and that is good because she needs support and someone with whom she can talk. What is she talking about in counseling? I would suggest she investigate how a second marriage differs from a first, and the importance of learning to accept her husband's attitudes toward his first family, not to fight them. Once she knows and accepts these attitudes, the second wife can help her husband as well as motivate him to enjoy his new relationship.

I also suggest she stop being competitive. Stop the rivalry with the ex-wife. Think in terms of a not-too-distant future when his former wife has finished college and his fourteen- and eighteen-year-old children are out of school. If the second wife lacks the patience to wait for her second marriage to ripen slowly, she can choose to learn *how* to be patient—how not to impose her ideas on someone who isn't listening, even though they may be very good ideas. Her request for criteria to judge the legitimate requests of an ex-wife and the reasonable meeting of those needs should be rephrased to read, "What can I do to motivate myself, and perhaps my husband, to improve our relationship?"

Fun in the Summer for Second Wives

Donna Bilbrey

Summertime . . . sunshine, backyard barbecues, swimming, and fun. For many remarried women, however, summer brings added responsibilities as well. This is often when noncustodial fathers have extended visitation rights with their children from previous marriages.

Whereas the fathers look forward to the priceless privilege of daily contact with their children, many second wives have mixed emotions about these extended summer visits. Though they share their husband's joys, stepmothers also are aware of what is involved in the daily care of these tykes. Laundry, dishes, and meals can increase tremendously. And if the stepmother is a nonworking wife, the children are constantly under her supervision while Dad is at work.

Aside from increased household chores, she will deal with new emotional issues on a daily basis. "My mom doesn't cook eggs that way!" "My mom always lets us eat our dinner in front of the TV!" "My mom! My mom! My mom!" A stepmother hears these statements and hundreds of similar ones everyday. She must continuously reaffirm to her stepchildren that she most certainly is *not* their mother and that things are done differently in the two homes.

The majority of stepmothers try desperately to live down the wicked stepmother stigma. Of course, they want their stepchildren to feel welcome during summer visits. At the same time, however, these visits can become trying. Regular daily patterns are interrupted. If the husband—unaware of the daily trials that the presence of one or more kids can create—fails to pitch in, his new wife may end up feeling used and taken advantage of. She may also feel stifled in airing her negative feelings about caring for these children. With her natural offspring, she would have no trouble declaring, "These kids are driving me crazy!" When it comes to her stepchildren, however, her feelings may get lost somewhere in her own thoughts, classified *unspeakable*.

Stepmothers should accept their negative feelings as normal. Their job often goes unappreciated. Few natural mothers thank a stepmom for taking such good care of her children. Most often, in fact, the stepmother is viewed as a rival—which is too bad, because kids benefit from the involvement of any loving adult.

Stepmothers need to approach summer visits with the lines of communications wide open with their husbands. Before the visit, wife and husband must sit down and talk over any expected problems and how they will handle them. The husband should be prepared to do his part with the household chores. Two of the most important things they should schedule are *time alone together*—perhaps an evening out for dinner or a movie without the children—and *time alone for the stepmother*. She should plan an afternoon with a friend or even a trip for the family's weekly shopping—as long as she goes alone. These simple plans provide for much-needed breathing space away from stepchildren.

If the groundwork is laid well before the visit, it will be an enjoyable time overall. The stepmother can relax and have fun getting to know her husband's children. She doesn't have to bend over backwards to please the kids. She should just be herself. She should say no when necessary, and yes as often as she can. She should let her conscience be her guide and remember that they are only children for a short while. Someday, when they are grown, they won't forget the part she played in their childhood and their summers.

5

Enriching Yourselves as a Couple

How Does Sex Fare in Second Marriages?

Frederic F. Flach, M.D.

Sexual conflicts commonly contribute to marital disharmony. Although men and women often attribute the death of a first marriage to sexual difficulties, these are usually not the only reasons their relationships failed. As most of us know, sex is a very sensitive barometer. It masks and signals problems in communication, understanding, power struggles, unresolved resentments, and sometimes simply the failure to integrate the more romantic and emotional aspects of marriage within the strains of everyday life.

Everyone considering a second marriage—or already starting one—is going to give thought to how sex will fit into it. If you have experienced sexual frustration or conflict in a previous marriage, this issue will be a particularly sensitive one.

Chances are that a couple entering a second marriage will have had more sexual experience than either might have had before their first marriage. Most likely, they will have explored their own sexual compatibility. Unless other factors, such as companionship later in life or social and economic benefits stemming from the structure of the new marriage, are primary motives, they will have concluded that sexual intimacy between them is acceptable at worst and superb at best.

Does a good sexual relationship prior to a second marriage or in its early stages carry a money-back guarantee? Can you count on it lasting forever? Hardly.

Here are a few guidelines to make your expectations more realistic and the likelihood of continued sexual compatibility greater.

A poor sexual relationship at the beginning is not likely to improve as time goes on. The chances are that one or both of you carry within you unresolved conflicts about sex, which are not likely to be *cured* just because you are marrying someone you may love and respect in other ways. Professional counseling may be indicated.

A good sexual relationship at the beginning will require thought, empathy, and planning if you want it to endure. Creativity is important, too. A story appeared some years ago in *The Washington Post* about a couple who had developed an imaginative strategy to keep sex alive in their marriage. About twice a month at around 2:00 P.M., the wife would drive to the center of town and pick her husband up on a prearranged corner. They would cross the bridge to Virginia, check into the Marriott Hotel, and make love. Afterwards, she would drop him at the same corner and go home. When he arrived later for dinner, he would toss his briefcase onto the hall table, walk into the kitchen, hug her, and, smiling, ask how she had spent the day. This parable points up the importance of creativity, humor, flexibility, and playfulness that characterize good sexual interaction.

Knowing how to communicate effectively, how to resolve conflicts and live with differences in perspective, and how to be empathetic and avoid carrying grudges is not specifically related to sex. But almost everyone knows that a deterioration in sexual closeness often reflects a disturbance in the nonsexual aspects of a marital relationship. Practicing good communication, tolerance, respect, honesty, the art of forgiveness, and the many other skills necessary to good human interaction is another matter, but it is also *essential* to giving your marriage a solid sexual quality.

Don't be misled by statistics or popular opinion. How often you and your new husband or wife make love is very much an individual matter. There is no more magic in four times a week than in four times a month. It's how sensually and emotionally fulfilling sex is that really counts.

Sex is unquestionably important, but no more so than the richness that grows in a good marriage and usually overshadows the importance of sex itself as the years go by. Being older and more experienced, having learned a great deal by this time, you should be much better prepared to make sex work for you, while keeping it in perspective, the second time around.

Do You *Both* Want a Child?

Claire Berman

Susan had never been married before she met Ken and became stepmother to his two children. She liked the youngsters, who spent alternate weekends and a month every summer with the remarried couple, and simply assumed that (when the time was right) she and Ken would add to the family with a child of their own.

Ken did not share this assumption. In this new relationship, he was looking forward to some freedom, to living somewhat spontaneously, to not being tied down as one tends to be with children. When Susan learned that Ken was unwilling to have a child, she was disconsolate.

The question of whether to have a child in a remarriage (in which at least one of the partners is already a parent) has no easy answer. Yet unless age and physical condition clearly preclude the remarried couple from becoming parents, the matter is likely to come up. Because so many factors come into play in reaching a decision, it is not surprising that husband and wife are apt to view the possibility of parenthood differently.

Consider the situation we've just described—one that is growing increasingly common. Men have many reasons for not wanting a child of the new marriage, and these reasons have little or nothing to do with their feelings of affection for the second wife. At the core of the problem, frequently, is the fact that husband and wife are at different stages of the life cycle, and each is responding to different needs. The men are likely to be older than their new wives.

(The median age difference between single women and the divorced men they marry is six years, as contrasted with a two-year difference for first marriages.) They have had their parenting needs satisfied and have found fatherhood a mixed blessing. (The fact that there were children may have added stress to the breakup of the first marriage.) The fathers may feel guilty if they live apart from their children, may be financially strapped because of obligations to those children, or may simply be looking forward to a quieter, adults-only life-style the second time around.

It's a long list of maybes, and an understandable one. Equally valid, however, are the new wife's feelings, especially if she has no children of her own. *Her* parenting needs have not been fulfilled; her maternal urge has not been satisfied. As one second wife put it, "I've given a lot of time and energy to my stepchildren, but they also have their mother. Who'll be there for me when I grow old?" Another stated succinctly, "I want one for my team."

Given the tensions that predictably may arise over the decision to have a mutual child in remarriage, it is surprising that so many men and women go into marriage without first addressing this issue. Timely professional help in resolving this conflict can be crucial to the success of the marital relationship.

Suppose, however, that husband and wife agree about having a mutual child. They may be concerned about the feelings that children of previous marriages will have toward the new baby. It is hard to predict what having "our" child will do to the couple or to any of "his" or "her" children. In general, family experts are optimistic. Sometimes, indeed, the new baby may serve to unite both families: the baby is the one thing they have in common.

Certainly, the question of whether or not to have a baby is not one to be posed to the other children. As in a first marriage, this important decision belongs solely to husband and wife. If having a child is important to the two of them, then they should plan on a mutual child. If it is not important, they should concentrate on other aspects of the relationship.

How Not to Let Guilt
Destroy a Second Chance
Frederic F. Flach, M.D.

Guilt is a potentially serious saboteur of second marriages. It is often insidious, unrecognized, and apparently without solution. The idea that you have no right to build a new life on the wreckage of the past can introduce a terrible tension into your life, undermining every effort to make your new marriage work. Guilt can spoil and destroy unless you know how to admit its power *and* have strategies to resolve it.

The first distinction you must make is between *legitimate* guilt and *unhealthy* guilt. Despite the fact that our society has tended to reject the concept of guilt in favor of self-fulfillment and self-gratification, the experience of guilt is an ancient, vital part of human nature.

Guilt promotes both the survival of the individual and that of mankind. Guilt, like pain, is a signal, warning us that we are on a course of thought or action that is destructive to ourselves or others. Guilt prompts us to atone and to modify our future behavior guided by what we have learned through regret.

Unhealthy guilt is essentially unwarranted guilt. For example, if you're the type of person who assumes that everything that goes wrong in your life and the lives of those around you is your fault, then this grandiose sense of responsibility becomes your Achilles heel; you react with guilt to all kinds of adverse events over which you have little or no control.

Guilt can also be unhealthy when it is beyond your awareness. During the first year of a second marriage, one or both partners can become depressed, turn against the other, find all kinds of flaws in their relations—even think of divorce—because of the destructive influence of guilt.

What can you do about it? Here are some guidelines that may help:

1. Accept, within reason, your own contributions to the failure of your previous marriage. This may hurt, but it is much more constructive than denying them. To put all the blame on your former

spouse prevents you from correctly appraising your own limitations and working to correct them the second time around.

2. By the same token, don't assume *all* responsibility for your past marital failure. Absorbing all the guilt can be blinding and demoralizing. Even if your former mistakes seem pronounced—negligence, angry outbursts, even an extramarital affair—you must accept the complexities of human behavior. You also may not have been mature enough to deal with the stresses and challenges marriage then demanded of you.

3. Acceptance sets the stage for learning. For example, if in the past you handled all conflicts either by giving in or by stubbornly refusing to compromise, modify your behavior this time around. If you sought to solve a sexual problem or your own fear of closeness and dependency through infidelity, this time concentrate on making trust and commitment the cornerstone of your relationship.

4. The greatest source of guilt is the inevitable trauma that affects your former spouse and your children. But obsessive preoccupation with the damage does little good. Rather, strive to put things right as quickly and surely as possible. Learn to forgive yourself and everyone else involved. Minimize legal wrangling if possible. Reassure small children that they still have two parents who can work together on their behalf. Create an atmosphere in which teenagers can count on joint parental guidance.

5. Finally, a sense of destiny helps. We human beings are fragile, to say the least. We make mistakes. Life is a series of reverses and resurrections. Faith, good will, and an effort to do our best is sometimes all we can expect of ourselves. As one of my patients put it so well: "My divorce was a disaster. Everyone suffered. For several years I struggled to overcome a gnawing sense of guilt, even though it often seemed quite irrational. Then, after I married again, Jennifer was born. She's four now. She's brought tremendous joy to me, to my older children, to everyone. Somehow I feel it was meant to be—that God, or nature, or whatever force exists to design our lives wanted Jennifer to be born—and the agony of all we went through was necessary to set the stage for her coming."

Denial Damages Chances for Successful Remarriage

Elizabeth Einstein

Denial keeps remarried families from becoming all they can be as soon as they can. It keeps people stuck.

Denial means avoiding or rejecting reality. This common defense mechanism helps people protect themselves from what is too painful to accept. But as with alcoholics who deny their drinking problem, it is only when remarried people finally move from denying painful issues to confronting them that they can begin to build successful stepfamilies.

Denial can work in several areas. Some remarrieds cannot acknowledge the need to grieve the loss of a former family. Rather than let go of the pain, they suppress the great sadness of such a loss. Such unresolved grief may be expressed as anger or guilt, directed toward a new mate or stepparent. Some adults deny the importance of their former spouses to their children's lives, making their relationships very difficult. When children of divorce have poor relationships with their biological parents, or no contact at all, they have far greater problems adjusting to remarriage and new parent figures.

Most destructive of all is denial of one's feelings. Although anger, fear, jealousy, guilt, and resentment are all normal in new step-families, denial of these painful feelings is a common way of dealing with the tension and anger that erupts when these feelings are not talked about among family members. Denial merely dulls the pain and postpones it; it cannot erase the feelings.

For remarriage to succeed, stepfamilies must move beyond denial. People want to deny feelings that seem to represent their darker side. It's a kind of self-protection. Jealous of the ex-wife? "Never." Resentful of child support? "Of course not. I knew about it when we married." And so on.

Once the feelings get out of control and lead to a crisis, remarrieds are even more reluctant to talk about them for fear of opening up still greater troubles.

The main reason many remarrieds deny their difficulties is that to confront them suggests the family is failing. To a person still reeling from the loss of a former marriage, this possibility may be too devastating to face. Denial thus becomes a survival technique. Remarrieds cross their fingers and privately hope things will eventually get better.

In fact, just the opposite is true. Feelings that remain unrecognized and problems that are denied only delay the stepfamily's chances for success, and continued denial can destroy remarriages. When people fail to communicate their feelings or resolve issues, denial triggers a chain reaction that moves remarrieds into crisis. Unfortunately, denial is quite common; most stepfamilies seem to move from confusion to chaos to crisis before things get better. But things won't get better until denial stops.

A *crisis* means a turning point. If this critical time is used as a chance to get help and make changes, the remarried family can move into a new passage of sharing and building closeness. If not, the process of denial and the unresolved crisis may end the remarriage.

Denial occurs during various phases of stepfamily development. It's especially common during the first stage—fantasy. Basking in the glow and excitement of another chance at family life, adults and children often believe they can function like the "Brady Bunch." Of course, they can't. Unless people have information in advance about blending two families, they do not know some basic realities of this process. Believing that love can conquer all, many remarried families remain blind to glaring problems and to another normal stage of stepfamily living: confusion. "What am I doing in a stepfamily?" many ask themselves as they try to merge two different ways of doing things into one. But rather than facing the pain and disappointment of unmet hopes and expectations, they deny problems exist. Confusion then leads to chaos.

If denial continues into this stage, eventual crisis is predictable. When feelings and issues remain unrecognized and uncommunicated, remarrieds are headed for trouble. Confronting denial is painful, but getting the issues and feelings out in the open is the only way to clear the air and begin working toward stepfamily stability.

Try these specific steps when dealing with denial:

1. *Create awareness.* Identify the reality that some stressful issues and strong feelings exist among family members. Admit your own

part and motive in continuing the denial. Imagine your own worst fear of exposure.

2. *Make new decisions.* Awareness alone is not enough. Family members must risk sharing their fears and feelings to air the issues that have been denied. Family meetings create a positive and safe environment for this activity. Support groups for remarried families are another place to ventilate feelings among others in the same situation. These groups help people realize they are not alone—there's nothing wrong with them. It's just a challenging situation until they face the issues head on. If problems are severe, it is important to confront them with the help of a professional who has been sensitized to the remarried family's special dynamics.

3. *Practice communicating.* To end denial once and for all, family members must continually share what is on their minds. Over and over, they must practice sharing feelings and communicating their thoughts about the special issues that come up in these complex families. For many, this is risky and threatening; for some, shared feelings mean acquiring skills in the areas of parenting or communicating.

Once remarrieds move beyond denial and gain information about the reality of stepfamily living as well as trust in the process of becoming a new kind of family, they can transform stressful relationships into special ones. The caring and concern that come from facing up to reality through honest communication will lead to a deep commitment among family members.

Are You Communicating?

Marie Kargman

What is the number one cause of marriage failure? The answer is: a breakdown in communication. Is the risk of a communication breakdown greater or lesser in remarriage?

In talking to remarried spouses and asking them to consider this question of greater or lesser risk, I find the answers almost as varied as the number of people who responded.

To some, being called by a former spouse's name is enough to start a small war. To others, this same event can be a source of humor and a catalyst to talk about "their" marriage—how it differs from the first or others. I say others because some remarried husbands and wives have been remarried three or four times.

Recently, my husband and I were having dinner with a friend and her new husband. In a pleasant exchange of conversation, the husband was telling a story about a past event that included a former wife. For a moment he hesitated, searching for a word, then finally said, "I have had so many wives I forget which one it was." We all just laughed—including my friend, his new bride.

My point is that remarriage must deal with complexities not found in a first marriage, one of them being a previous sharing of intimate kinship. Although a present husband or wife may say and honestly believe a dissolved marriage is dead, the mind sometimes intrudes with uncalled-for ideas, feelings, or judgments about a former spouse and imposes them on the present marriage. Like all slips of the tongue, they just pop out. They aren't meant to be part of the conversation. They aren't intended to be a communication—but they very often are.

What Is Communication?

Ideas, feelings, and judgments are the substance of communication, of talking and responding, and of conversation. For talk to be *communication*, it must be directed at a particular person—a listener who either expects to respond or who, because of his or her relationship to the talker, is expected to respond. This *give-and-take* expectation makes the interchange a conversation rather than a lecture.

Lectures may be a good one-way talking exercise in a classroom, where both teacher and student agree that the teacher talks and the student listens. Students respond only when asked, usually in an exam. In marriage, however, lectures are not usually a form of communication.

That is not to say that lecturing by one partner and a delayed response, perhaps the next day, or the next week, or even later, is an uncommon experience in marriage. Very often the lecturer mistakenly thinks he or she is engaged in a communication. I doubt that there exists a marriage counselor or therapist who has not heard this complaint: "I talked about that until I was tired, but he never had an answer. Two weeks later, out of the blue, we were discussing another subject and the answer I expected two weeks ago became the new topic of conversation—unrelated, unasked for, and certainly making no present sense!" It is safe to say that a lecture followed by a delayed response is one variety of breakdown in communication in marriage.

Expectations and Misunderstandings

Married partners expect that their talking will be listened to. They expect that the response of the listener will make sense to the original talker, so that they agree there is understanding between them. When two people agree they understand what is being talked about, they are communicating. You may ask, then, why there is so much misunderstanding when married people speak to each other? Just listen to the common response, "I didn't say that!" or "I didn't mean that." A person sometimes wonders how he or she could be so misunderstood!

The simplest statement between husband and wife can never truly be simple, because every communication in a marriage takes place simultaneously on three levels of understanding. Each verbal act (talking is a verbal act) sends a message along three communication pathways: (1) the *idea* path, a *thinking* process; (2) the *feeling* path, an *emotional* process; and (3) the *judgment* path, a *moral* process. And each verbal message is received on all three pathways: idea, feeling, and judgment. Thus a single spoken sentence can elicit any one of nine possible responses, with eight possibilities for misunderstanding.

Since the listener must choose to open the response with one out of the possible nine replies, the chance for error is great. Although a listener may be aware of many possible replies, an individual can talk about only one level at a time.

On What Level Are You Talking?

Let us discuss the dilemma of one couple, Jack and Susan Adams. Susan says, "You didn't pick me up when you said you would."

Does she mean she was wondering why her husband was delayed? Or was she annoyed because she was kept waiting? Or is he a *liar* who never keeps his word? Jack replies on the idea level: "The car didn't work, and I had no way to contact you." If he has guessed right, the partners have had a respectful communication. She wanted to know *why*; he told her, she was satisfied, and that unit of interaction was over. *Why* is a request on the *idea* level. But if Susan was annoyed with Jack for being late and expected him to respond to her feelings of unhappiness, an answer about the condition of the car would be no answer at all.

What could Jack say to show that he got the *feeling* message? He could say, "You are annoyed with me for being late and I don't blame you." Although it might not satisfy Susan't unhappiness, from a communication point of view it would put both talker and listener on the same wavelength. But if Susan is telling Jack that he *never* keeps his word, then Jack would be obligated to reply with words that would tell Susan he is aware of her *judgment*, that he hears it.

Now you can see why it is not uncommon for marriage partners to discover they aren't talking about the same subject, or on the same level. Sometimes it becomes necessary, before responding, first to find out if you understand what kind of reply is expected by the person who began the conversation.

Hauntings
Frederic F. Flach, M.D.

A James Thurber cartoon shows a man identifying a woman crouched on top of his bookcase as his first wife, suggesting how former husbands and wives may literally haunt a new life, exerting an ongoing and frequently disruptive influence.

Of course, if you were married only a brief time and had no children together, your first partner will probably disappear from your life. You may remain friends, but more often you will have little or no contact with each other as the years pass. If you do happen to meet, at a party or an airport, your encounter may resemble the chance meeting of casual acquaintances.

If, however, you have been married for some time, and especially if there are children, your relationship will most likely never end. The children themselves will remind you—by a physical resemblance, a gesture, a way of talking—of the person with whom you once shared a life.

Although the nature of the residual relationship with a former spouse can vary greatly, most seem to fall into a few typical patterns. In the most enviable of all, you may find that you and your former husband or wife have remained friends throughout; or that, although you were once enemies, you have regained some respect and liking for each other and so have entered into a more comfortable relationship. Or you may find, unfortunately, that you are perpetually at odds with each other.

If the third circumstance applies, you should formulate a kind of foreign policy of conduct toward a former husband or wife. Your ultimate purpose is fourfold:

To prevent the former partner from draining either your emotional or material resources

To prevent your relationship with your former husband or wife from having a detrimental influence on your new marriage

To keep any ongoing hostilities or manipulations from hurting your children

To try, if possible, to restore or maintain some semblance of respect between you and the person with whom you once shared a marriage

How can you accomplish these ends? There are certain time-worn principles, derived from painful experience, that you should observe.

If the financial or legal structure that was drawn up is clearly inequitable and hence repeatedly provocative—a husband paying a punitive amount of alimony or a wife never knowing from month to month whether the money to which she is entitled will be coming—try to get this straightened out. Granted, it is not easy; but an arrangement that was set up in anger may lend itself to improvement when tempers cool and resentment subsides.

If there are ongoing hostilities, however, they will show up—through critical and unfair remarks made to children, through total noncommunication, through routine calls to discuss a simple matter like visitation arrangements that end in bickering and hanging up. If this happens, consider two things. First, what is the source of the hostility? Second, what can you do to reduce it or at least to keep it contained? The origins will determine, in no small part, the solutions.

If the hostility you encounter from a former husband or wife is rooted in insecurity (because the world on which he or she depended has been rudely shattered) or in vindictiveness (because of feelings of rejection), time is on your side. As your former partner settles down, creates a new life, becomes accustomed to being apart from you, and finds new interests, the chances are good that reasonable communication and some of the old mutual respect will return. In such a case, try to handle contact with your former mate with some degree of compassion and tolerance. Stay in touch. Avoid arguments. Do not respond in kind to provocations.

If the hostility toward you stems from deeper sources, your strategy will have to be quite different. It is one thing to have had a number of good years together and then find your marriage falling apart. It is quite another to have been engaged in arguments, long days of silence, power struggles, and other forms of warfare throughout your marriage. If what has happened since your divorce and remarriage is only a continuation of what was going on for years before, there is little reason to expect it to change. Here, as a rule, the less contact you have with each other the better. With no resolution possible, it is pointless to go out of your way to please or accommodate. Moreover, you may have to use quite a bit of firmness and ingenuity to set limits on your former partner's behavior, refusing to take the bait and be stirred up by provocative remarks, and insisting that he or she live up to the terms of your separation agreement. Sometimes the best thing to do is simply to be unavailable when he or she tries to reach you on the phone.

This policy of noninvolvement is especially important if your former husband or wife is paranoid—not in the sense of having full-blown delusions but by showing a tendency to distort what you say and how you behave. One cannot reason with such unreason; if you attempt to do so, you will find yourself gradually being reduced to a state of confused and angry immobility.

Even when there is no such open combat, there are other negative maneuvers that call for different precautions. A former husband or wife may, for example, reach out in a dependent way, looking for emotional support and asking for guidance. By all means offer it, but be careful not to encourage the kind of involvement that leads to undesirable consequences. There are two common dangers: First, you may delay your former partner's development of a life of his or her own. Second, you may compromise your relationship with your new partner.

It is essential for those in a second marriage to behave in such a way as to make it eminently clear that the new relationship comes first.

Part of your commitment to your new marital partner includes a willingness to help him or her cope successfully with a former mate. If indicated, you should help your husband or wife set intelligent limits on the disturbing behavior of a former partner. Be careful not to encourage any petty vindictiveness or anger that will only aggravate the situation. It is far more constructive to encourage an end to the unnecessary guilt that is all too common after divorce. Try not to engage in misplaced jealousy; remember, the chances are excellent that if your new husband or wife still had any real feelings of love left toward a former partner, he or she would still be living with that partner, or at least the two of you would not be married. If there were good years together in a former marriage, as is often the case, then there is bound to remain some element of affection and memories of good times together, but this should offer no threat to the current relationship.

Facing the Feelings Remarriage Brings and Letting Go

Elizabeth Einstein

Feelings influence all relationships, and if feelings become intrusive, they must be faced in order to restore harmony. This is especially true in new remarriages. Because of the complex web of relationships and unresolved emotions among many family members as they seek adjustment to one another, negative feelings may run rampant.

Fear, anger, jealousy, guilt, and resentment are all part of a remarried family's emotional heritage. So are hope and joy. Feelings are neither right nor wrong; they simply *are* and need to be acknowledged. Negative feelings are healthy emotions that signal something is awry, out of balance. Jealous of the former spouse? "Never." Resentful of child support? "No, I knew he had to pay it." Guilty because you don't love his children? "No, if I try harder, the love will come."

Such clues can help restore harmony among your stepfamily members—if you pay attention to them. Let's look at some specific, common feelings people in remarriages experience.

Fear: The Deadly Stopper

Fear can paralyze the normal process of remarriage.

A fear of the past repeating itself is often harbored in the hearts and minds of adults as well as children. Since both have already experienced the pain of ending a family, fear of this happening again sometimes keeps people immobilized. This fear may keep family members from investing their total energy and resources in the stepfamily's future. They may hold back, reluctant to commit themselves totally. When this happens, the remarriage gets stuck in a stage of confusion or chaos until a crisis forces change, which either ends the remarriage or stabilizes it.

Guilt: Keeper of the Conscience

Guilt—the feeling you have done something wrong—serves as a double reminder. We have failed our own ideals, or we have not fulfilled a commitment to others. Guilt is often present when people have *not* prepared for remarriage by letting go of the past or by examining their own expectations about remarriage.

Guilt seems to be a common denominator among family members. Some people left marriages even though their former mates did not want their marriages to end. Some people feel guilty for disrupting their children's lives. Children might even believe they had a part in the marriage ending and blame themselves. And although everyone in a new stepfamily might be feeling guilty, *no one* talks about it. Unresolved guilt tends to damage self-esteem. When unresolved guilt continues, family members cannot channel all their energies into new relationships.

To lighten emotional overloads, remarrieds need to distinguish between real and imagined guilt. Real guilt comes from breaking commitments or doing things to hurt others. Imagined guilt comes from taking responsibility for something that you need not—for the behaviors or feelings of others. For example, if your stepchild steals something, you might feel guilty because you feel you somehow caused the child to act that way. Or you might feel that you "should" have been able to stop him. Though you blame yourself, the reality is that your stepchild's behavior reflects the values and upbringing he received in his first family and in no way is your fault.

Guilt has a positive side, too: it causes people to be responsible for their behavior. When you make mistakes, hurt people, or intentionally wrong someone, guilt haunts you until the wrong is rectified. If you use guilt feelings as a signal that you have transgressed in a relationship, it can guard your goodness. As guilt motivates you to make amends, you can confront the family member and right the wrong. Besides restoring the relationship, releasing guilt is the beginning of forgiving yourself. Confronting guilt is a painful struggle, but releasing it can stabilize a remarriage.

Anger: The Disrupter

Bottling up anger is costly. Yet too many remarrieds do just that. They're either unaware of why they feel angry, or they simply deny it. Adults may harbor anger from the past or about what they may not be getting in the present. If you have not clarified issues with your former spouse, each time you deal with him or her about the children your unresolved anger might resurface. It might affect interactions with your children or stepchildren, or you might project it onto your new spouse. Children might be angry about their losses because they had no choice about what happened to them. They live within a new set of relationships because of their parents' choices, not their own.

Anger can be an instinctive response to the frustration of goals and needs. If you didn't deal with hidden agendas and clarify your expectations before remarriage, your needs probably are not being met. When stepparents feel rejected or unrecognized by their stepchildren, anger can breed resentment.

Resentment and Jealousy: Relationship Destroyers

Jealousy is closely associated with competition. In a remarriage, where time and money must be shared with so many people, both adults and children might feel jealous. There always seems to be a shortage, and loss has a way of creating extra needs.

Like jealousy, resentment often results from having to share resources. It is a frustrating emotion. Although you can identify and understand certain situations as part of reality, you may still resent them. Resentment can make people grouchy, sullen, moody, vengeful, or retaliatory with family members.

Denying feelings is a common way to deal with difficulties arising in new remarriages. But denial merely dulls the pain; it doesn't eliminate the feelings or clarify the situation. Too many remarrieds deny their negative feelings because they fear that talking about them will stir up greater troubles. Actually, just the opposite is true. Unrecognized and unshared feelings can topple your remarriage. Dealing with feelings honestly, on the other hand, can help bring the family closer, building a stronger family unit.

Letting Go of Difficult Feelings

Once you decide to move from denial to confronting the painful feelings, you are on your way to freeing yourself from them. There are some specific things you can do to let go of the feelings that keep you tied to the past.

1. *Recognize the feeling.* Face the feeling fully. When it emerges, don't push it away in an attempt to feel better: the relief will only be temporary. Stay with it and take the time to truly identify the feeling. Locate it in your body: my stomach aches, my head hurts.

Find an image that matches how you feel or attach a color to it—red. Give the feeling a name—*anger*.

2. *Express the feeling.* State the feeling aloud, to yourself or to another person: "I am feeling angry that my husband seems to forever side with his son."

3. *Clarify the feeling.* Stay with the feeling and look deeper to see what's really behind it. If you are feeling angry at your mate, there also may be, beneath the anger, a level of sadness or disappointment that your efforts are not enough to get your stepchild to respond positively. Your dream of being the *perfect stepmother* may be already shattered. Or you may feel guilty about not measuring up. Whatever, clarify what the feeling really means to you and be sure to look at its many faces.

4. *Explain the feeling.* As you have the courage to go deeper into exploring the feeling, you might identify a reason underlying it. Beneath that anger you might harbor a deep fear, rooted in your childhood. Perhaps there was a time when one of your parents sided against you and you felt left out, rejected. What you might be feeling today is the same thing you felt as a little child. When you can actually identify and explain the feeling's source, you can begin to respond with a new behavior.

5. *Accept the feeling.* Since there is no value placed on feelings—they just exist—you are neither good nor bad because you feel a certain way. None of us can control what we feel from day to day. When you stop judging feelings, you stop judging yourself. Then it is easier to accept the feelings—and yourself for having them. You will also find it easier to accept the feelings of others as well.

When you use this process to confront difficult feelings, you will experience the freedom of leaving them behind. Taking time for resolving feelings and saying goodbye to those hurting parts within yourself will change your attitude and your behavior, giving your remarriage a real chance for success.

Vasectomy Reversal

Jane Mickelson

The fact that my husband Don and I could conceive a child together still seems to us to have been a very special miracle. After the birth of his second child with his first wife, Don had made the decision to have a vasectomy, not knowing that the marriage would end before a year was out, leaving him the single parent of a three-and-a-half-year old daughter. We met, fell in love, and discussed marriage, but were worried about what effect not being able to have children together might have on our relationship.

I was thirty at the time and felt very strongly that I wanted a child, so when we heard about a reversal operation, called a vaso-vasostomy, Don immediately looked into it and, before long, went to Yale–New Haven Hospital and had the surgery performed. Seven months after our wedding, we conceived a baby. Our son Jared was born in March 1977, healthy and beautiful—the perfect addition to our family. It all sounds so simple, yet it involved months of highly emotional soul searching on both our parts, as well as concerns about what we should do if the operation were not successful. At that time, in 1975, the odds were not in our favor. The surgeon who performed the operation told us that there was about a 20 percent chance that the reversal would work. Fortunately, Don's age and excellent state of health were highly beneficial factors, and the skill of the surgeon was an additional advantage.

Vasectomy, the sterilization of the male, is a simple, relatively minor surgical procedure. From start to finish, including preparation of the site to be operated on (the scrotum) and time for the commonly used local anesthetic to take effect, a vasectomy done by a practiced physician takes little more than half an hour. Done in a doctor's office or in clinics on an outpatient basis, the operation is practically painless. First, the area is shaved and anesthetized; then a small opening is made in the scrotum, the skin that encloses the testicles. The *vas deferens*, the tube that carries sperm from the testicles to the urethra (the tube through which a man ejaculates) is located and then pulled out through the incision. The sheath of the vas is opened, exposing the vas itself. This is then cut in two, and the ends of the vas are sealed off in one of several ways. They may be sealed by ligation (stitches), either doubled back onto themselves and then sutured onto the vas itself, or with the ends buried in the surrounding tissue, or with the sheath of the vas pulled over the cut ends to form a barrier. Another method used is electrocoagulation, in which an electric needle is inserted into the cut ends of the vas and used to cauterize them. This forms a hard scar, which seals the ends of the vas. A final method, one that was thought at one time to be more easily reversible, is the application of tantalum clips. (Tantalum is an inert metal, which cannot harm human tissue.) It has been found, however, that the damage done to the vas by the clips, which turned out to be highly difficult to remove, makes this method no better for reversal than any other. Once the vas is securely closed off, the sheath covering it is replaced and the scrotal incision is closed. It is most common to use absorbable sutures such as catgut, since there is more risk of infection with nonabsorbable sutures, which must later be removed.

Most couples who choose this method of contraception are very happy with it. Side effects are generally rare and can be corrected. Infection can occur, as can sperm granulomas. The latter are non-bacterial abcesses consisting of sperm, lymphocytes (white blood cells), and epithelial cells (sloughed off from internal mucous membranes). They occur when the sperm leak into the surrounding tissue and can occasionally cause the man mild to severe pain. Unfortunately, channels can open up through the granuloma, thereby creating a new passageway for the sperm and returning the risk of pregnancy. The chances of this happening, however, are minimal, and although a significant percentage of vasectomized men do develop these granulomas, most of them are totally unaware of their presence. Whether or not the appearance of granulomas has any effect on the subsequent success of a reversal is an issue that is still under debate.

Before his vasectomy, Don had been counseled, both about the operation itself and about the possible emotional and physical after-effects. At that time he was told that it was a permanent operation, as reversals are by no means predictably effective. Most counseling sessions cover in detail each step of the vasectomy, as well as emphasizing the need for contraceptive use until it has been determined through a lab test that all sperm are absent. Because of the uncertainty of reversal, no doctor should ever suggest vasectomy as a temporary form of birth control. We were extremely lucky, but there are many cases in which reversal has not worked.

Vasovasostomy, or vasectomy reversal, is a far more difficult, lengthy, expensive, and uncertain operation than is a vasectomy. In the United States approximately 2 out of 1,000 vasectomized men request a reversal, although many doctors feel the demand would be higher if the operation were more widely publicized. The reasons most men give for wanting a reversal are primarily remarriage after divorce or death of spouse, death of one or more of their children, a previously unexpected desire to have a larger family (generally after a major improvement in family finances), or, very rarely, problems dealing with the vasectomy, either psychological or physiological. This last reason accounts for fewer than 10 percent of all the requests.

The reversal operation must be done in a hospital with highly trained personnel, and even then there are no guarantees. It cannot be stressed strongly enough that the success of the reversal is heavily dependent on the technique of the original vasectomy, as well as on the way in which the surgeon reconnects the *vas deferens*. If too much of the vasal tissue was damaged by the original operation, then chances are that it will be impossible to reconnect the ends of the vas, or that the connection will be under too great a strain and will separate at a later date. If the vasectomy was performed too low in the scrotum, reversal is far more difficult to achieve, as it is also in the case of a single-incision vasectomy, rather than the standard method in which an incision is made on either side of the scrotum. The less vasal tissue removed, the better, from the viewpoint of a later reversal, since this will leave the surgeon with more tube to work with, so that the removal of scar tissue will not shorten the vas to the point of strain when reconnected.

There are two methods of performing a vasectomy reversal, each taking between one and a half and three hours. The surgeon must reopen the site of the original vasectomy and remove the scar tissue from the ends of the vas, which are then realigned and reconnected. This is not as easy as it sounds, since there has often been swelling of one end of the vas, as a result of pressure from sperm blockage. The doctor also checks to make sure there are sperm in the fluid coming from the testicles, and must sometimes remove more of the vas until sperm are found to be present; their absence can be an indication of a blockage further up the vas, and this must be removed.

The first of the two techniques for performing a vasovasostomy is called the *macrosurgical,* since it does not usually employ the use of a microscope, although many doctors will use a loupe (similar to a jeweler's loupe) or a magnifying glass. This method involves using a fine nylon monofilament to align the open ends of the vas while the outer, muscular layer of the vas is sutured (stitched). The filament is removed within a week or two. The need to leave an opening in the scrotum for the filament may permit bacteria to enter the incision, which can cause infection. It may also occasionally be necessary to reopen the incision to remove the filament. The second method used is done with the aid of a high-powered microscope and is called the *microsurgical* method. It uses finer suture material and involves reconnecting both layers of the vas, first the mucosa (the inner layer) and then the muscular (outer layer). The incision is then sutured shut. Although the microsurgical reversal seems to have a slightly higher success rate than the more conventional macrosurgical operation, it is also longer (requiring more anesthetic) and consequently more expensive, as well as employing more expensive machinery, which the hospital must purchase and maintain. The microsurgical method also demands that the surgeon be trained to work with this equipment.

Very few men have side effects from the reversal operations. Fewer than 10 percent suffer from complications with the anesthetic or with hematoma (swelling due to collected blood in the tissues). Most doctors suggest that the need for physical support of the testicles will continue for two to four weeks. Their recommendations for abstinence from lovemaking are somewhat more variable, ranging from ten days to four weeks. Some physicians feel it is important to use contraceptive methods until the quality of the renewed sperm can be tested. The potential effects of damaged sperm (which may occur for a while after a reversal) on the health and well-being of a conceived child are not known precisely, but it certainly makes sense to err on the side of caution. On the other hand, some doctors feel that if a couple wish to conceive, they should do so within a year or two of the reversal operation since in some cases the vas has disconnected as a result of stress at the site of the reconnection, or has built up scar tissue that blocks the passage of sperm.

The success rate of vasovasostomies varies widely. Although certain doctors claim a 100 percent success rate of returned sperm, not all of these men were then able to impregnate their wives. The age and health of the man has some significance, as does the technique used for the original vasectomy. Another very important factor seems to be the amount of time that has passed between the two operations. Recent studies have found that virtually all men who had reversals within two years of their original vasectomy resumed a completely normal sperm count. In men who had their reversals within ten years, the figure was 91 percent, but it dropped dramatically to only 35 percent for men who had their vasectomies more than ten years before their reversals.

In other cases of failure to return to a prevasectomy sperm count, damage to the nerves of the sheath of the vas may sometimes be the cause. If the nerves of the vasal sheath are destroyed, contractions of the vas, which move the sperm through the urethra, cannot take place. Research indicates that permanent damage to the sheath can occur if too much of the vas was removed in the original vasectomy, if a suture or a clip was applied too close to the sheath, or if there was severe inflammation after the first operation. The formation of an abnormal amount of scar tissue can also cause sheath nerve damage. Buildup of sperm antibodies, which occurs after a vasectomy, has been suspected of reducing fertility in the man even after his reversal. Although men with higher levels of sperm antibodies in their blood tests achieve fewer pregnancies, there are a number of cases where the levels of antibodies dropped after the reversal operation took place, and some cases in which they rose, so high antibody levels are not necessarily a reason to reject this operation.

When my husband had his reversal operation, studies were just beginning to surface concerning the effects of vasectomies on coronary heart disease. It had been noticed that test animals that had been vasectomized tended to have more coronary heart problems. These studies must be held at least partially responsible for the decline in vasectomies performed over the last decade, although research compiled since that time has shown no such increase of coronary heart disease in vasectomized humans. It was theorized that there was a connection between the buildup of sperm antibodies and the buildup of arterial plaque (deposits in the arteries), leading to the hypothesis that these antibodies form clusters which then deposit themselves on the walls of the arteries and contribute to atherosclerosis (blockage of the arteries). So far there is no conclusive evidence on either side of this issue; yet there seems to be, from the studies that have been compiled, no noticeable increase in coronary heart disease in the male population that have undergone vasectomy.

One unusual and unexpected side effect of sperm antibody buildup that has been noticed concerns nucleoprotamines, which are a normal component of human sperm cells. Antibodies increase to reject and destroy these nucleoprotamines in the vasectomized man and fight against the sperm that his body must absorb each day. He is, therefore, far more likely to have a severe allergic reaction to a medication called protamine, which is commonly used during operations to reverse anticoagulation drugs. If the patient is aware that this situation can occur, he can inform his doctor that he has had a vasectomy, and the side effects of the protamine can be offset with a preparatory administration of antiallergic drugs.

How successful is vasovasostomy? Again, it is hard to be exact, especially since follow-ups of men who have had the reversal are few and sketchy. But the odds are improving all the time as doctors become more familiar with microsurgical techniques, as these techniques are refined, and as more people hear about the possibility of reversing their vasectomies. Depending on which doctor's statistics you read, pregnancy rates have ranged from 16 percent to 85 percent—a wide range, to be sure. It must be assumed also that a doctor with a high percentage of successful reversals will be more likely to publish the results than will one with a low success rate. Overall, however, in younger men whose vasectomies took place recently and were cleanly done and free of major complications, the odds are not bad.

So many circumstances in a person's life can change drastically from one stage to another. Major decisions that made good sense at one time can cause heartache and regret later. For Don and me, the blending of our lives and love into the person of our child was one of the greatest miracles of our marriage. Yet without the medical technology made available to us, this miracle would have remained an impossible dream. For others in the same position, I can only hope that sharing our experience will give them enough knowledge to make a thoughtful decision, and one that is right for them.

How to Choose a Surgeon
Angie Pallow-Fleury

Almost any urologic surgeon is willing to do a bilateral microscopic vasovasostomy or vasectomy reversal. You must decide what your priorities are and select a surgeon with whom you can work and feel comfortable. We began our selection process by interviewing prospective surgeons by telephone. In these interviews we asked questions that dealt with the issues highest on our list of priorities, thereby narrowing our field of prospects. We then made appointments with three of the most likely candidates for a more in-depth interview, a physical exam, and a final selection. We had the surgery done after much ado, research, and many problems, in August 1984. Here are some of the questions and conflicts we encountered:

How much experience has the surgeon had with this procedure? How frequently does he or she perform this procedure? How many operations has he or she performed? We were told to look for a surgeon who has done the procedure many times and on a regular basis. It is also possible that some physicians, after performing this surgery many times, may become overconfident and have a tendency toward sloppiness, whereas a physician with somewhat less experience may be more careful.

What is the surgeon's success rate? Most of the physicians we interviewed claimed not to know their statistics regarding outcome. They did tell us that the average sperm-return rate is about 75–90 percent and that the rate of conception is about 25–50 percent. We were also told that the success rate declines steadily in direct relation to the number of years it has been since the vasectomy was performed. Thus, the best reversal potential exists one year or less following vasectomy. Ten years or more after vasectomy, the chances for reversal are very poor.

What procedure is used? We discovered a controversy regarding method of reversal. The most common method involves straight resection of the *vas deferens,* with microsutures used inside the lumen, as well as on the surface of the vas. The other method involves cutting the vas on a diagonal and suturing only the outer surface of the vas. This second method is not considered true microsurgery by the physicians who use the first method.

Is the operation performed on an inpatient or outpatient basis? Individual physicians have their preferences. Most of those we talked with use the outpatient surgery option. Since most insurance companies do not cover this elective surgery, cost may be a major factor in discussing this question with your physician.

What is the average duration of the procedure? This may depend largely on the experience of the physician. We received figures ranging from one hour to four hours of actual time in the operating room.

What options are available for anesthesia? This was a major concern or ours in planning our reversal surgery, since I believe anesthesia is the most dangerous part of any operation. Local anesthesia seemed to be the most logical choice, as the actual incision is only about one inch long and the vas lies relatively close to the surface. What we had not considered was the duration of the operation and its delicacy. It is done under a microscope with 40× magnification, so any slight movement resembles an earthquake. Lying perfectly still for even an hour is difficult, if not impossible. Some physicians are more flexible on this issue than others. If you and your physician do choose a general anesthetic, remember that you now have another physician with whom to consult: the anesthesiologist.

What drugs are used routinely? Even with a local anesthetic, we were told that intravenous valium would be given. With a general anesthetic, routine preoperative medications would be ordered. We were told that antibiotics were contraindicated because they promote scarring. A prescription for postoperative pain medication is also routine with most physicians.

What are the routine postoperative orders? These will differ somewhat depending on whether the surgery was performed on an inpatient or an outpatient basis. Most doctors prescribe the constant wearing of an athletic support for one to two weeks and recommend no vigorous physical exercise for two to four weeks. We were given no instructions regarding follow-up or sperm counts after the operation.

What are possible complications? Aside from anesthesia and surgical complications, at least two major problems can affect the success of the reversal. The first is scarring, which can constrict the flow of sperm through the newly resected vas. The second is a sperm–antibody reaction in which antibodies are produced that render the sperm immobile or actually kill them. Some physicians believe that in some cases these conditions are only temporary.

Ideally, you should give yourselves as much time as possible to set your priorities, select a physician, work out all the details, meet with the anesthesiologist, and familiarize yourselves with the operating room facilities and staff. If you want to deviate *at all* from standard operating procedure, be prepared to spend time and energy coming to an agreement between hospital administrators, boards, physicians, anesthesiologists, and nursing staff.

6

Learning to Be a Stepparent

Coming to Terms in Stepfamilies:
What to Call the New Mom or Dad

Claire Berman

Stepmother. Stepchild. The titles that designate relationships in families formed by remarriage are often weighed down by myth and mistrust. Who has not read about Cinderella's wicked stepmother, and who has not heard the description, "He was treated like a stepchild"?

No wonder, therefore, that men, women, and children in stepfamilies are reluctant to use these relationship terms and, instead, spend a lot of their time and emotional energy on the issue of what to call each other.

Should the woman in the house who assumes the duties of caring for her husband's children be called Mom? Stepmother? Aunt? Is it appropriate for the stepchildren to call her by her first name? What about the stepfather? If he takes over most of the responsibilities of a father, should he be called Dad? And should the actual parent require the child to acknowledge the incoming stepparent by the use of a formal relationship term? These are some of the questions stepfamilies grapple with.

Here is what typically happens. Assuming the first marriage has been severed by divorce, remarriage writes an end to the child's fantasy that Mommy and Daddy will get back together. This is the time when the child must mourn the end of the first family and must resolve his or her feelings of betrayal, anger, and divided loyalties. Uncomfortable with calling the stepparent Mom or Dad, the child generally avoids using any title at all. "Meet my 'er' . . . " is the way a stepparent is likely to be introduced.

Often, even those children who *would* like to call their stepparents Mom or Dad are stopped from doing so by the knowledge (understood or declared) that the real parent would view this as supreme disloyalty. "I'm just waiting to hear my son call my ex-husband's new wife Mother," said one angry woman. "That will be the ultimate violation."

Adults can help children by letting them ease into the new extended family and making it clear that the relationships rest on a good deal more than choice of titles.

What *can* stepfamilies do to come to terms with terminology? Many adults find it helpful to step in slowly and let the child know what *is* acceptable. "You may call me Howard," a stepfather might say. If he is uncomfortable about being on a first-name basis with a child, he may find a different appellation acceptable. "Why don't you call me Mr. J?" It is a nickname that has stuck and is used with warmth in this family. It works because, as a nickname, it designates a close, insider relationship, but it does not intrude on the existing bond between the child and his father.

Some youngsters have found it a simple matter to call their father Dad and their stepfather Pop. Although both describe a paternal connection, there is no conflict, for the two men (father and stepfather) do not answer to one and the same term. Finding a similar compromise for mother and stepmother is more of a challenge.

Different children in the same family may refer to their stepparent differently. It is not uncommon, for example, for younger children to address the heads of the custodial home as Mommy and Daddy, regardless of actual biological ties, whereas an older child is likely to be more self-conscious about terminology. Each child should be permitted to follow his or her natural inclination without being corrected.

Youngsters in stepfamilies must be assured that it's not what you call a person, but how you feel about someone, that's important. Adults, too, would do well to keep that in mind.

Stepping into Parenting Someone Else's Children

Patricia L. Papernow

Becoming a parent to a new partner's children can be more challenging than any of us bargained for. "I wish I'd known more about what to expect," said a young woman named Pam in my office the other day. She had married a wonderful and loving man—but she had also married his children! The kids, a teenager and a ten-year-old, had been friendly enough when Pam and George were dating. But, "When they cried through our entire wedding, I should have known it was going to get harder," Pam said, laughing through her tears. "If only someone had helped us to be more realistic, maybe I could have gotten down to working things out much earlier, instead of spending two years feeling depressed and inadequate!"

The following suggestions for people in the process of becoming stepparents are drawn from Pam's experience and from my own background as a stepparent and a psychologist involved with stepfamilies:

1. *Take a deep and honest look at your fantasies and yearnings for this new set of relationships you are about to enter.* Your fantasies may go something like this: "If I work hard enough, the kids will love me"; "I'll be a better parent than my partner's former spouse, and the kids will be so grateful"; "Our new family will erase the hurt of the previous divorce/death"; "Our kids are all about the same age, and it will be fun for them having stepsiblings."

If you see yourself in any of these statements, you have plenty of company. A person entering any new relationship brings his or her particular set of yearnings and fantasies. (For mental health professionals, the fantasy is: "We understand this, so it will be easy for us!") For remarried families, the wish for the new step-relationships to be nourishing and satisfying from the start is normal and universal. Fantasies become problematic only when their hold on you prevents you and other stepfamily members from working on the realities inherent in early stepfamily life.

2. *Move in slowly.* Stepparents, especially full-time stepmothers and stepfathers, often expect (and are expected) to step immediately into a parental, nurturing or disciplinary role. To expect children to accept you in such a role so quickly is to invite disaster. Children will respond with outright hostility, passive resistance, or (at best) indifference.

The transition will be easier for everyone if you begin with reality: you are strangers foisted upon each other, and you need time to get to know each other. Take time to find out who your stepchildren are. As distasteful as it may feel, in the beginning think of yourself as a disciplinarian only in the absence of the biological parent, much in the role of babysitter: "Your father says these are the rules and it's my job to enforce them while he's gone." For a while, make requests for change through your spouse.

As you get to know each other better, it will be more appropriate and, in fact, necessary for you to step in directly when taking disciplinary action, with your spouse's support. But as painful as it is, you must begin as an outsider!

3. *Learn as much as you can about what the kids are feeling.* Children come to stepfamilies with a history of loss and change beyond their control. They have experienced a troubled marriage or a painful death. They have lost their family. They have learned to live in at least one and often two single-parent families.

Although the presence of a new adult on the family scene may provide some relief for the child in a single-parent family, it also creates yet another loss. The stepparent bumps this child from his or her intimate relationship with the biological parent. Evenings that were spent snuggling with Mom watching television are now spent alone. The living room, which had become a comfortable place to lounge around, is now off limits for food or mess because the new stepparent prefers a more formal room.

Although no one enjoys the rejection and even outright hostility that often greet stepparents, understanding that your stepchildren are struggling, too, can help you approach the situation with empathy. As Pam said, "It would have helped me so much to know that my stepchildren's temper tantrums each time we went out were normal, and [were] their way of dealing with yet another loss, not just a mean attempt to keep my husband and me apart. Not that they weren't trying to do that! It's taken us two years to figure out that we need to arrange some special time for John to be alone with his children each week, rather than giving up our time alone together or going out and fighting about it."

Finally, understanding your stepchildren's need for distance and their resistance to you does not mean you have to tolerate abusive or nasty behavior. Civil behavior is a reasonable expectation. The trick is to state your needs while still acknowledging the child's feelings: "I know you're not real pleased to have me here. You don't have to love me or even like me. But I do need some of the basics! I need you to look at me and say hello when I walk into a room." A variation of this theme is: "I know there have been a lot of changes in your life, and this new arrangement is not easy for you. But I would like you to answer my questions and not turn your back and walk out of the room. I will do the same for you."

4. *Pick a few things to change.* As you get to know your stepfamily and get clearer about your feelings and needs, satisfactions and dissatisfactions, there will be *many* things that make you uncomfortable. When you feel ready, choose one or two things that really matter to you. What you choose is less important than finding one or two things that would make a difference to your sense of comfort and belonging in the family. It may be regular time alone with your spouse, no noisy stereos after 10:00 P.M., or a door on your bedroom. A full-time stepmother may want to ask that her spouse reclaim some of his parental role. Another stepparent may finally decide he wants to attend a school conference.

Stepparents do need to make changes in the family routine in order to feel at home. Understanding your stepchildren's needs and feelings about change does not mean giving up your own. It does mean going one step at a time. And it means acknowledging that when we ask children to endure yet another change over which they have no control (even if it's as minor as using their silverware differently), we are asking a lot. So choose a very few things that mean a great deal to you and let the rest go for awhile. (Complain about those things you've left unchanged to your friends or a stepparent support group.)

Understanding your stepchildren's feelings also requires that children, especially teenagers, be included in the decision-making process as new rules are set. Adults may have the final say, but children need to feel their needs have been heard and seen.

You will need your spouse's support to pull off any change. Your chances of getting this support will be greater if you state your needs without implying that the child is "bad." "My mistake," said Andrea, "was that I would ask for Bob's support with his daughter by ranting about what an ungrateful and spiteful child she was. No wonder he got so defensive! Now that I have a baby of my own, I understand how painful that must have been for him. Lo and behold, when I said something like—'This is painful for me and I know she doesn't mean it, and would you help me?'—he's much more supportive."

5. *Resist the urge to compete with your stepchild's biological parent.* One of my clients, a thirty-year-old woman whose mother died when she was twelve, said of her father's second wife, "My stepmother was really smart. She told me over and over again that I had a special place in my heart for my mother . . . a place that would always be there and nothing would change it. I don't know how she knew, but by doing that she helped me understand that I could make a different space in my heart for my new stepmother. I sure gave her a hard time, but I have come to love her fiercely and I am grateful that she helped me do that without giving up my mommy."

6. *Prepare yourself to be an outsider.* Your new spouse and his or her children have an older, closer, and in some ways much more intense relationship than you will have with either of them for awhile. Your job and your spouse's, over time, is to build your new step-relationships so they are nourishing and satisfying. Meanwhile, your partner and his or her children will agree with each other more than you will agree with either of them. They will turn to each other when things are hard. They will protect each other more than they will protect you, leaving you with an uncomfortable set of feelings—jealousy, resentment, inadequacy, and loneliness. Although these are nobody's favorite feelings, you can take solace in knowing you are responding normally to a tough situation, and you are not to blame. "The worst part was not the jealousy," said Christine. "The worst part was feeling so badly about myself for feeling that way!"

7. *Stay involved with your most important interests outside your new family.* In the early stages of your stepfamily life, while you are still on the outside, nourish friendships beyond the family. These friends

will provide the strokes that are not yet forthcoming from your stepchildren. And work that you love can provide the sense of mastery that may be missing in the early interactions with your spouse. It also may give you the necessary strength and clarity to return to the struggle after a disappointment. Although it is important to spend time with the new family, spending hours watching your partner and the kids play games you hate (ones they've played for years!) will leave you feeling resentful, deprived, and downright foreign. Take some time away to do something by yourself or with friends for part of the children's visit. This may provide you with more energy to deal with them when you return.

8. *Start immediately to develop a stepparent support system for yourself.* In my research on stepparent development, the better the level of support, the more quickly and painlessly stepparents can establish a satisfying role within their new family. Stepparents who, in the early stages, have someone to talk with who understands their feelings and can help sort out what they want, can move as much as eight years more quickly through the developmental process of creating workable new step-relationships.

Find other stepparents; join support groups or start your own; read as much as you can; learn about normal stepfamily development; and get help figuring out what you feel and what you need to be more comfortable. Whether it is time alone as a couple, help in disciplining a stepchild, or the simple acknowledgment that your painful feelings are real and understandable, support that helps you feel clear about your needs will greatly improve your chances of meeting them.

9. *Learn as much as you can about your spouse's feelings.* It is clear that the best source of support and the best guarantee of developmental progress toward a well-functioning stepfamily is a couple relationship where partners can accept each other's painful feelings and fears with empathy and curiosity. Life will be much easier for you if you are one of the rare stepparents whose partner can hear and accept your feelings of jealousy and frustration as well as your needs for couple time alone, right from the start. Likewise, your spouse will be much more cooperative if you are a stepparent who can empathize with your partner's deep connection with his or her kids, as well as with the difficult middle position in which your demands place your partner.

Most couples find that this kind of empathy takes a while to develop. The problem is how to hang in there until you understand and hear each other. When your new partner greets your tentative expressions of discomfort with disbelief or criticism, it may help to remember that biological parents often find a stepparent's negative feelings disturbing and even terrifying. As one newly married father said, "I thought, 'Oh no! If she doesn't love my kids, how are we ever gonna make this thing work?' "

When your spouse can't hear your feelings, then you need to know that he or she probably needs more support from you—for example, "This must be hard for you to hear," or "Did that scare you?" Clara, a woman who married a man with three kids who visited them every other weekend, said, "I struggled for a year to tell him I wanted some time alone with him while they were here. The weekend was our only time together. He would tell me I was being selfish, and then I'd withdraw and get depressed. Finally, it occurred to me to ask him what it was like *for him* when I asked for time alone. He said he felt incredibly hurt. That he wanted us to be a family, that he had so little time with his kids, and that it felt like I was asking him to disown his children, that I had time with him during the week and why couldn't I let go of him during the weekend?

"Instead of defending myself, for once I *repeated back* what he said to me: that he felt really hurt and maybe scared. You know, he started to cry! Something changed after that. It was like we were more on the same team trying to figure out a hard problem: how to give him the time he needed with his kids and still give me and us time alone, together. We came up with this neat idea that the Thursday night before weekends when the kids come, we would have a *date*. When we were poor, it was pizza and watching 'Hill Street Blues.' Now we go out to a nice restaurant. We also take at least one walk together while the kids are here. It makes such a difference!"

10. *Work on your couple relationship.* All our research so far says that stepfamilies *can* make it even if stepparent and stepchild do not get along. Stepfamilies *do not succeed*, however, unless the adults in the family become a cooperative, mutually supportive problem-solving team. Take regular time alone together without the children, even if it's only breakfast or a walk after supper. Learn to listen to each other when you disagree.

As outsiders, stepparents often feel the need for adult couple time more acutely than their partners do. Just as it is the biological parent's job early in the relationship to make sure the children's needs are met, it is the stepparent's job to pull gently but firmly on the biological parent for time alone together, without kids.

As the stepparent, remind yourself that the biological parent is in the middle and may often feel torn. (As the biological parent, remind yourself that the stepparent who is an outsider needs your attention and support to feel comfortable. Also remember that nourishing your couple relationship is *crucial* to the success of your new family. When hard-won solutions don't work, spend your energy figuring out what you learned for the next time, rather than fighting over who was to blame.)

11. *Get help if you need it.* Couples in stepfamilies begin their lives with many more forces pulling them apart than first-time-around families. Good couple or family therapy can make the difference between painful, ugly struggles with no resolutions and a healthy, safe, satisfying family life. Ask around to find someone who knows something about stepfamilies or someone with whom several other people have had a good experience.

If you find the latter but not the former, bring your therapist a few things to read about stepfamilies. Also feel free to look for someone new if the first person is not helpful. It is especially important that therapists working with stepfamilies *not* take sides, but help both adults or all members of the family see what each does to make things worse, and what to do to make things better. If your partner won't go to couples therapy, drag him or her to the nearest stepfamily support group in your community.

Becoming an effective stepparent sounds very hard, and often it is! Membership in a stepfamily does force couples to work much more intensely at the beginning of their relationships. My own experience is that although it sometimes takes extra help to learn to work well together over highly charged stepfamily issues, those who succeed have forged vital, nourishing, and enduring relationships.

How to Work with the Other Parents

Claire Berman

This was to have been an article about "How Mothers and Step-mothers Can Work Together (and Why They Should Attempt to Do So)." Three paragraphs into the original draft, however, I came to a stop. It suddenly occurred to me to ask: Why am I placing the responsibility for cooperation and communication solely on the *women* involved in the complex extended families created by the marriage–divorce–remarriage sequence? In continuing to focus on the woman as creator of harmony or discord in a family, am I not perpetuating the kind of myth that leads to fears of the wicked step-mother? Shouldn't the attainment of successful relationships be regarded as the responsibility of both the women *and* the men who are involved with them?

This, then, is about how mothers and fathers and stepmothers and stepfathers can work together (and why they should attempt to do so).

The *why* part is easy. It's good for children to witness civility instead of contention among the grownups who are supposed to guide them. Parents and stepparents who frequently argue or who refuse to talk to each other tend to use the children as message bearers. They need intermediaries to carry on communication that remains necessary because of their continuing connection through the children. The role of message bearer is a difficult one, however, and one in which children are inappropriately cast. The adults in both households must make an effort to communicate directly with each other.

It also is helpful to learn what the expectations for behavior are in that other house (whether it is the custodial or the visited home), so you can establish some consistent expectations for the children's behavior.

Peggy chafed because her twelve-year-old stepdaughter Lisa did no chores in her home, even though Lisa spent three days of each week with her father and stepmother. Each day after leaving her office, Peggy would stop at the store to buy groceries, go home to prepare dinner and set the table—while Lisa talked on the phone with her friends or watched television. When Peggy complained, her stepdaughter insisted that she *never* had to do anything at her mother's home. After dinner, Peggy or Lisa's father cleared the table and washed the dishes. One day, when Peggy decided she'd had more than enough, she picked up the telephone and called Lisa's mother. "This is Lisa's stepmother," she announced to the startled woman at the other end. "Would you please tell me what your daughter is responsible for when she's with you?"

Lisa's mother replied, "She sets and clears the table and washes the dishes. She has to keep her own room clean."

"Now," says Peggy, "Lisa handles those chores at our place, too. And I have it on very good authority that I've not made unreasonable demands upon the child."

Peggy's phone call also opened up communication with Lisa's mother, with the result that information is exchanged more frequently and smoothly between the two households. Everyone has benefited.

Granted, consideration and cooperation are often more difficult to achieve when the remarriage of a former spouse is new. "As a parent, one has to confront feelings of jealousy toward your child's same-sex stepparent," says Diana Richter, a New Jersey family counselor who is herself a parent and a stepparent. "It helps to understand and believe that the bond between parent and child is extremely strong. Although a child may love another adult, the biological parent can never be replaced. When one understands this, the need to compete disappears and many positive possibilities begin to open up." One of these possibilities is a recognition of the important roles played by all of the parent (and stepparent) figures in the child's life.

It helps if you can see things from the other person's point of view. Richter offers a personal illustration: "As a stepmother, I typically felt very unappreciated at times for all the things I did for my stepchildren. I realized that it was unrealistic to expect thanks from children, but the feeling of wanting thanks was there. Recognizing this helped me to appreciate the effort my own children's stepmother expended on their behalf. I decided to let her know that I appreciated what she did for my children. I believe this confirmation that she was a valued person in my children's lives led to an even better relationship between them, and I feel comfortable knowing that they are well cared for at their father's house."

Here is another example of how and why it's helpful to work with the "other family." "When I moved to a new home with my new [second] husband," says Florence, "the children came home from school with the usual cards requesting two names of people who could be contacted in case of emergency. Having no relatives close by, I thought of neighbors. But I was uncomfortable with putting down names of people who barely knew my children. It occurred to me that there were other people who were equally involved, concerned, and invested in my children—my former husband and his new wife. They wholeheartedly agreed to be available. They are another resource for me as well as for my children."

David clearly remembers the first time he viewed his son Seth's stepfather as an asset. "Seth was having trouble in school," says David. "We thought it might help him to work on a computer, so we bought one. But I'm all thumbs when it comes to anything mechanical. Seth's stepfather, on the other hand, is a computer whiz. In fact, it bothered me to hear Seth talk about all the things his stepfather could do. Finally, I put my pride aside and phoned the man. He came over the next evening and set the whole thing up. Now, when Seth has a question about the computer, he phones his stepfather—even when I'm within earshot. I've become much less resentful of the influence this other man has on my son's life."

But what if contact is more difficult to make? One woman who became an instant parent when she married a man with children found herself faced with a situation where her new husband's relationship with his former spouse was extremely tense. They couldn't have a conversation (in person or by phone) that didn't end poorly. Yet this young woman felt a need to communicate with the mother of her stepchildren. She initiated a relationship through correspondence, writing notes to ask the children's mother's advice about issues that concerned them. By keeping all of her contacts with the biological mother focused and respecting the mother's primary relationship with her own children, the stepmother minimized the threat she might have presented while also opening the door to improved communication. Such efforts represent an important first step for *everyone* in the family.

Guidelines for Stepfathers
Frederic F. Flach, M.D.

Stepfathers play a crucial role in the lives of the children they inherit in second marriages. The extent of a stepfather's involvement with his new wife's offspring can vary extensively—from a casual friendship with her grown children and their families to a significant replacement for the real father in cases where a former husband fails to maintain contact with his own youngsters.

Being a stepfather is often not an easy role to assume. Your influence on your stepchildren—their values, behavior, and emotional health—can be profound, whether they are very young or already in adolescence. You are the man in the house, a model for them and a counterbalance to their mother's foibles, just as she is to yours. The *first* rule you must observe is to be well intentioned and honest, and to avoid harming those entrusted to your care.

Unless their real father has essentially vanished and you find yourself confronted with a situation comparable to adopting the children as your own, you will have to take on many of the day-to-day responsibilities of fatherhood without really being the father. So, *rule number two* is: remember you are not the real father, nor are you under most circumstances a substitute father. That's one reason that so many stepchildren call their stepfathers by their first names, or simple Uncle. The term conveys affection and respect but reserves the title Father for its rightful bearer.

What does this imply for guidance and discipline? *Rule three* is not to compete with their real father—for love, for control, for authority. Nor should you, on the other hand, abandon altogether any valuable input you can make toward their personal development. For example, try to avoid criticisms that unnecessarily put their real father in a compromising light. He may not be as well off financially as you are, or he may be more so and a potential target of your envy. He may not spend as much time with the children as you think he should, but they undoubtedly value their contact with him and can only be hurt or resentful at comments that deprecate the efforts he does make.

Do not hesitate, however, to stand for reality. Don't permit yourself to engage in covering up grave deficiencies—such as serious alcoholism, abuse, or negligence—in their real father if such exists. You do the children no favor to encourage potentially damaging illusions. At the same time, you can significantly complement his contributions. He may be reliable in paying child support but ineffectual in offering personal or career guidance. He may be loving and supportive but simply unable to help them financially in ways that you can.

Assuming you also have children of your own from a previous marriage—or even your new one—*rule four* is: do not confuse your stepchildren with your own. The relationships are usually different by their very nature. To deny this reality can be a source of confusion for everyone. You can love your stepchildren and be a wonderful friend to them, but you should never feel something is lacking in your makeup if you cannot have the same sense of fatherhood you feel toward your own. In fact, you sometimes may have to reassure your own children that your fondness for your stepchildren (who may live with you, while your own children do not) does not compromise your basic relationship with them.

Expect some areas of real conflict and misunderstanding, and be prepared to deal with them. You and your wife may not entirely agree on certain principles of child rearing. She may believe in strong discipline, while you may prefer to talk things out. She may have a casual attitude toward schoolwork, whereas you may think the children should study harder in order to get into good colleges. Perhaps you think children should be seen and not heard, whereas she thinks they make an important contribution to family discussions at the dinner table.

Rule five calls for recurrent mutual exploration of such attitudes and of potential sources of conflict with their mother as they arise. You can certainly learn more from each other, and when there are irreconcilable differences you can decide how to live with them. You do not want to permit such tensions to eat away at the foundation of your new marriage.

Remember that each family has a personality of its own, just as every individual does. Your new marriage is not simply a sum of all the people involved. A new, dynamic life force is created among all these people; it must have something to work toward—an overall strategy, a dream. Being an effective stepfather is one of the tactics required to achieve that dream.

Eight Problems Common to Stepfathers

Clinical reports suggest stepfathers have a set of common problems unique to their role. These conclusions, however, are based on interviews with a limited number of stepfathers and do not represent all stepfather family functionings. If you find yourself experiencing some of the feelings and situations described here, you should know you are not alone and that you can reconcile many of these difficulties.

1. *Uncertainty about the amount of authority in the role of father:* The transition from a friendly relationship with children before marriage to a parenting one is uncomfortable for stepfathers.

2. *Uncertainty about the amount of affection to give stepchildren and ways to show it:* Stepfathers say they feel uncomfortable kissing their stepchildren and do not always like playing games with them.

3. *Disciplining stepchildren and enforcing rules:* Conflicts arise between stepfathers and their wives over what is and is not important to enforce. When stepfathers criticize their wives' children or attempt disciplinary action, mothers suddenly become protective of their offspring.

4. *Money conflicts:* Some stepfathers must satisfy the financial demands of two families. Often the way they allocate money becomes a measure of love and devotion among stepsiblings and spouses.

5. *Guilt over leaving children from a previous marriage:* Guilt sometimes prevents stepfathers from giving openly to their new wives and children.

6. *Loyalty conflicts:* Stepfathers whose biological children live with their mothers sometimes regret the time they spend with their stepchildren. They feel this way because they spend so little time with their own children.

7. *Sexual conflicts:* The incest taboo is not as strong in stepfamilies as in biological families. Stepfathers may be sexually attracted to stepdaughters, stepdaughters to stepfathers, stepmothers to stepsons, and stepsiblings to stepsiblings.

8. *Conflict over surnames:* Some stepfathers strongly object to sharing their surname with their stepchildren, whereas other stepfathers want to adopt their stepchildren under their names.

Unfulfilled Need or Malicious Intent?

David A. Baptiste, Jr.

Mr. and Mrs. P. came to therapy four and half years after remarrying. Each spouse's first marriage had ended in divorce. Each had one child. Mrs. P. had a ten-year-old daughter, Meg, and Mr. P. had a sixteen-year-old son named Sam. Our first meeting together focused on Sam's disrespect for Mrs. P. and his uncooperative behavior as the family prepared to move to Boston for a sabbatical year.

Mrs. P., who did not work outside the home, was in charge of the day-to-day preparations for the move. Sam objected to this move; he feared not having friends and not being happy in Boston. Mrs. P. felt that Sam's behavior was reflecting negatively on her competence. As a mother, she was unable to manage Sam. As a homemaker, she was behind schedule in the moving preparations. Three and half years earlier, when Sam had first joined his father's family, he and Mrs. P. had experienced many conflicts. Mrs. P. perceived these current difficulties as an extension of their earlier problems. She demanded that something be done about Sam, "even if it meant sending him back to his mother."

Mr. P. felt caught in the middle. He wanted to please both his wife and his son. He also felt his wife was making too much of Sam's objections. He was confident that, once in Boston, Sam would adjust satisfactorily. However, he did not want to rock the boat by pushing Mrs. P. to "lighten up" on Sam. "She had graciously consented to let him come live here," he said. "She did not have to do it! They had their problems then, but survived. I feel this too will blow over." Despite his low-key attitude, he was concerned about the quality of his marital relationship and the effect his son's and Mrs. P.'s differences were having on it. There was a noticeable deterioration in the relationship between Mr. and Mrs. P. as well as between Mr. P. and his son.

A primary contributor to this situation was Mrs. P.'s insistence that Sam return to live with his mother, even though she knew that was not possible. Mrs. P. argued that she had given Sam her best shot and it had not worked. She said she would not take Sam to Boston unless he guaranteed to change his behavior. She wanted to "enjoy her year in Boston" and felt that she couldn't do so if Sam was with the family. Mrs. P. continuously rejected all compromises and restated her demand that Sam return to his mother. Mr. P. said that was not possible. Sam's biological mother had sent him to live with Mr. P. because of mother-son conflicts, and Sam could not return to his mother's.

At that point, everything seemed hopeless. Mrs. P., convinced that Sam's objections to the move were a personal attack on her, was unyielding in her demand that Sam leave the family. She was not open to hearing other explanations of his behavior. Finally Mr. P. shed some light on the situation. He revealed that since his divorce Sam had moved four times. The move to Boston would be number five. At each move, Sam had experienced difficulties in adjusting. Mr. P. felt somewhat guilty for "putting him through that by divorcing his mother, but it could not be helped." Many of Sam's adjustment problems resulted from the teasing he endured because he was overweight and aggressive in school. Although he had since lost his excess weight, he continued to be aggressive with his peers.

It was now clear that Sam's objections to moving were related to his fear of moving and were not intended maliciously to harass his stepmother. I asked both parents to put themselves in Sam's place and imagine how the thought of moving again would make them feel. This struck a responsive chord in Mrs. P., who had grown up in a military family. After much discussion and negotiation, Mr. and Mrs. P. began to understand that children in remarried families, like adults, are affected by the *ghosts* of previous family experiences. I invited both parents to change their approach to this situation. Rather than concluding that Sam's objections to the move were designed only to harass his stepmother, it was important for them to see his behavior in the context of his needs as an adolescent—an adolescent whose family stability had been tenuous at best, and problematic at worst.

As illustrated by this family, many remarried families seek therapy because of stepparent–stepchildren conflicts. Often it is the child rather than the adult who is perceived as the culpable party, the one whose behavior the therapist is asked to *fix*. Closer examination of the conflict, however, often reveals that whereas the child's overt behavior is worrisome, it is certainly neither malicious nor premeditated as the affected parents may believe. Because of past parent-child conflicts, parents frequently have difficulty in understanding the current conflict in its context. They often conclude that the child's intent is to harass the stepparent simply because he or she *is* a stepparent. With this attitude, parents are initially closed to hearing additional explanations for the child's behavior and remain convinced of its malicious intent. The stepparent then rejects any compromise short of removing the child from the home. Predictably, such requests are vetoed by the biological parent, and the entire family is in conflict.

For these families to overcome their impasse and resolve their difficulties, it is important that parents learn to view each conflict in context, rather than jump to conclusions about the child's behavior on the basis of past experiences. The context in which a behavior occurs is as important as the behavior itself.

It is also important for parents to be open to alternative explanations for a child's behavior. Look beneath the obvious. Ask questions designed to clarify the situation, and resist the temptation to view the child's behavior as a personal attack. More important, parents need to acknowledge and respond to a child's acting out as symptomatic of an unfulfilled need, rather than of malicious intent.

Do Fathers Really Want Stepmothers to Influence Their Children's Lives?

Frederic F. Flach, M.D.

The question of stepmothers' influence touches on one of the most sensitive issues in second marriages. Most fathers feel the pull of divided loyalties between the children of their former marriages and their new wives, as well as between children by their first and second marriages. This situation is often a far from painless condition. The more conscientious the father, the more he is affected by the situation as he struggles to define just how much influence his new wife will have—or how much he wants her to exert—on the lives of her stepchildren.

The opportunities for such influence are too numerous to list fully. Some of the more obvious come to mind. Your little boy or girl—age ten—is visiting for a week during the holidays. What time will he or she go to bed? How much television is permitted? Are children expected to eat all the food placed in front of them, or can they have a say in the day's menu from time to time? Can you give them an allowance, and if so, how much? How rigorously should they be punished if they do something wrong? Will they be returning to public or private schools when the holidays are over, and who will be paying the tuition?

Issues both large and small arise. Often, as children grow older, the concerns expand proportionately. Should children work and earn money during the summer vacations? What about a trip to Europe with classmates and under the supervision of a teacher during their senior year in high school? Where will they attend college? What career direction should they consider? How much should you attempt to influence them in their choice of schools, their relationships with contemporaries, their values? After graduation, should they go on to seek specialized degrees, or would it be better for them to go to work and earn money? Who will pay the bills? Should you buy them a car? If they're emotionally distressed, should you encourage them to go for professional help? Who will pay the bill? Are they ready to marry?

As the issues grow larger, so do the costs. When you consider your new wife's role in choices affecting your own children, you must distinguish between those options that involve money and those that do not. The former are inevitably greater sources of conflict and disharmony than the latter, unless you are one of those rare individuals for whom financial concerns are immaterial. Marriage involves sharing, and sharing invariably involves money and tangible assets. How much can you give or spend on your children without compromising your new marital relationship? How much say should your new wife have when decisions about your children affect your pocketbook?

There is no simple answer. Theoretically, decisions involving costs should always be shared. But what do you do if your attitude toward money varies significantly from that of your new wife? What if she objects to your expenditures on the basis of inappropriate emotions, such as jealousy or general insecurity? At times you may have to stand your ground and act independently. If you must act independently, however, be up front about it—avoid deception even if you risk controversy. There may be times, also, when she is absolutely right. You may be inclined to spend more than you can afford, or you may be influenced more by guilt than by good judgment. It's up to you to learn how to distinguish between those opinions of your wife's that are biased and those that are valid.

The most valuable contribution your new wife can make to the decision-making process is a fresh and different point of view. You may feel that because they are not her children, she may not understand or be appreciative of their needs. Sometimes this is true. More often, however, she will prove mature enough to offer you a set of values that can counterbalance your own as well as enable you to compensate for your own blind spots. Most of the time, two heads are really better than one.

Assuming that your value systems are not diametrically opposed—in which case you probably should not have married each other at all, because conflicts will appear throughout the matrix of your relationship—she can contribute a good deal. For example, you may overestimate the academic potential of one of your children; she may help you to see that you are pushing too hard and doing damage in the process. Conversely, you may not recognize a talent that one of your children possesses; she may point it out, helping you make crucial educational choices for the youngster. She may offer solace when you are too punitive, firmness when you are too indulgent, realism when you walk the edge of impracticality, imagination when you can find no solution to seemingly hopeless issues.

Of course, in most second marriages there is another person to be considered: your former wife, your children's real mother. She too will normally enter into the decision-making process, so there are often three (and, if she has remarried, sometimes four) parental figures in the picture—not to mention the child. One adult may have a vigorous antipathy toward any form of dependency; another may unduly encourage delays in a youngster's emancipation; still another may be indifferent to such issues. You may be left with the need to sort out conflicting inputs to arrive at a consensus or at least a point of view your youngster can comprehend and deal with successfully. It is sometimes a challenge to your skills at diplomacy and your mastery of group dynamics, both disciplines being well worth developing in any event.

No two people ever agree entirely all the time. Children will be exposed regularly to contradictory attitudes. One hopes these can be kept to a reasonable minimum. You want your children to be able to trust that your motives, intentions, and judgments about decisions made on their behalf are valid, and that your actions and those of their stepmother are guided by love and concern for their present and future well-being.

How Parents Intensify Sexual Feelings between Stepsiblings
David A. Baptiste, Jr.

Society disapproves of sexual relationships between closely related family members such as parents and children or brothers and sisters. In any family, the discovery of a sexual relationship between brother and sister is worrisome and stressful for parents. In stepfamilies, however, because of the nonbiological and nonlegal structure of the step-relationships, discovery of a sexual relationship between stepsiblings can lead to marital and family conflicts, even to family breakup. Sexual relationships between siblings—biological and step—are not unknown. Current research reveals, however, that opposite-sex adolescent stepsiblings tend to be sexually involved with each other much more frequently than opposite-sex biological siblings.

Biological siblings, who have known each other since their respective births, have had time to develop and put into place the incest taboo that regulates distancing between family members. Usually stepsiblings do not have this much time to develop the incest taboo. They share only a close social and spatial tie that has potential for emotional attachment to grow over time.

Absence of the incest taboo in stepfamilies can lead to the loosening of sexual boundaries and even to sexual involvement, although this occurrence is not automatically true. In many stepfamilies, parents often ignore the warning signs that indicate stepsiblings may be sexually involved or are defending against sexual feelings for an opposite-sex stepsibling. Signs of sexual stirrings between stepsiblings are often seen as conflict, and conflict is equated with failure. Because of the parents' fear of failure, they exert tremendous pressure on each other as well as on the children to *avoid conflict* by *instantly loving* each other in order to become an *instant family.* Conflicts such as territorial fights or fights that defend against sexual stirrings are quickly suppressed, since they threaten the family's fragile cohesion. Many parents openly deny but secretly acknowledge that sexual relationships between siblings, step or biological, are possible. These parents contribute unwittingly to such relationships by expecting opposite-sex pubescent stepsiblings to become closer friends than is usually expected of opposite-sex biological siblings.

In my experience, remarried parents are much more bothered by a distant relationship between opposite-sex stepsiblings and may push these children together. Observations of biological, opposite-sex siblings reveal that these children rarely share as close a relationship as that which parents in remarried families expect for opposite-sex stepsiblings. Furthermore, observations of adolescent development do reveal that relationships with opposite-sex siblings usually vacillate between relative closeness and absolute detachment.

The Cohen* family illustrates some of the problems that may occur when the parents' desire for family togetherness clouds their ability to see the warning signs of a sexual relationship between opposite-sex stepsiblings

The Cohens had been married three years. Each brought two children to the marriage. She brought a girl age sixteen and a boy age ten; he, two boys, ages nineteen and twelve. The discovery that nineteen-year-old Alan had been having sex with sixteen-year-old Carol brought the family to therapy. For the first eighteen months of the marriage, Alan—then sixteen—and Carol—then thirteen—fought incessantly, verbally and sometimes physically. Their hostilities had begun to spill over to the younger children. The antagonism between these two children concerned their parents enough that they insisted the children cease and desist their hostilities and become friends. Indeed, much to their parents' delight, they became

---

*The family name has been changed in this example.

inseparable. The parents congratulated themselves at their success in bringing tranquility to the family. Three weeks prior to entering therapy, the parents returned unexpectedly from a weekend trip and discovered Alan and Carol in bed together, which they learned was not a singular incident. Predictably, they were shocked and outraged. Mrs. C. blamed Mr. C. for Alan's actions. Carol commented, "Well, you wanted us to become friends. How much closer can we get?" Mrs. C. and her children left the family's home for a week.

When a sexual relationship between stepsiblings is discovered, it is best for parents to respond calmly and to assess the circumstances that fostered the relationship. Unfortunately, parents tend to blame each other and fail to assess their possible contribution to the situation, wittingly or not. Parents need to:

Discuss the situation with the involved siblings.

Resist the temptation to blame any one sibling. Usually the male is held culpable.

Establish new and explicit rules for the siblings' future interaction.

Consider therapeutic assistance if all in-house measures fail.

Keeping Sexual Stirrings between Stepsiblings in Control

To reduce the likelihood of a sexual relationship developing between stepsiblings, you need to:

1. Be aware that it is possible for a sexual relationship to develop between opposite-sex stepsiblings. Be prepared to discuss this possibility with each other as well as with the children.
2. Be especially careful that you do not encourage or provide opportunities that allow development of a sexual relationship between opposite-sex stepsiblings.
3. Discuss the *facts of life* with all pubescent children, biological and step, of both sexes.
4. Encourage all children, especially females, to inform parents when another sibling, biological or step, touches or fondles them in a manner that displeases them.

5. Allow children to verbalize their sexual fantasies about an opposite-sex stepsibling without fear of recrimination from biological or stepparents.

6. Resist the temptation to push opposite-sex stepsiblings, especially adolescents, to become closer friends than they want or can tolerate at that time. Encourage children to develop their own friendship networks inside and outside the home.

7. Accept as *all right* the usual intersibling hostilities, which are common to all families, without attempting to discourage or suppress such activities as unacceptable.

7

Strengthening Your
New Family

Building a New Identity
as a Stepfamily
Jamie Kelem Keshet

A stepfamily is composed not only of individuals, but of minifamilies as well: the parts of the former nuclear family that resulted from divorce or death. For example, a mother and her children or a father and his children form a minifamily. When a stepfamily is first formed, the minifamilies are likely to have more distinct identities than the stepfamily as a whole.

It takes time, often as long as three to five years, for a stepfamily to connect into a strong unit with a sense of identity. It takes time for nuclear families to develop as well, but that happens in a way we call natural as children arrive and grow up slowly. In the stepfamily, suddenly, there you are.

The first task of your family life is to *accept each other* and the fact that you are all members of the family, at least some of the time.

The next stage involves establishing the *authority* of the couple as the executive system of the family, and the ability of each adult to set limits for and offer guidance to each of the children. Although your new identity is being built as you go through these stages together, you may be in too much pain and shock to realize it.

The third stage of stepfamily life—*affection*—is when you reap the benefits of the prior two. This is when you begin to discover that there are new bonds holding all of you together.

A New History

New experiences that you share as a stepfamily bring you closer together and also make new history, to be recalled later. In our family, my teenage stepson introduced us to a water slide near Lake Winnipesaukee several years ago. Although he has now outgrown vacationing with the rest of us, we make our yearly visit to the water slide and always remember his contribution to this tradition. When we see him, we report the improvements in the slide, again building our common connection.

You can use the time you've already spent together to create a sense of identity. Maybe that Fourth of July picnic last summer was a disaster: it rained, two of the children had a fight, and drinks were spilled all over the garage floor. As miserable as you all were at the time, you were all there. You may be able to recall it with a smile or to use it as a metaphor, "I hope Joey's birthday isn't another Fourth of July picnic." It becomes an in-joke, a reference with special meaning for your family.

Recognizing the children's growth and development is another way of evoking history and connection. Remind your stepson as you strain your neck looking up at him that he was only up to your shoulders when you first met. Take out the first birthday card he signed for you, and show him how shaky his handwriting was.

Holidays, vacations, and special occasions like birthdays or graduations are important markers for remembering family history. In stepfamilies these times are often confusing and sometimes conflictual as complex arrangements are made to share children. Your holidays may seem more like a survival test than an identity-building time. If you consciously think of them as a time to build family identity, however, you and your partner may be able to create new family traditions.

One family chose to celebrate Christmas a week early in their household to ensure a calm, relaxed day, rather than have the children there for part of the day as they had in the past. Another family resolved an argument between two stepsisters over whose mother made better birthday cakes by buying an ice cream cake for the six-year-old's big day, which started a new tradition in their stepfamily. The stepbrothers and stepsister in another family decided to sleep out in the backyard during the week they were all together at one home. Because they had such a good time, they repeated the adventure year after year. This activity became part of their stepfamily identity.

New Space

The space your family uses at home and in your community is also part of building your new identity. If you are all living in the home that once belonged to one of you, you may want to fix it up differently as a home for *all* of you. Planning and making home improvements can bring you together as a family. Your new decor reflects your stepfamily's tastes as well as your ability to work together.

Finding special places in your neighborhood also builds identity. There's a certain corner of the park where you play ball together, a favorite pizza shop, a dilapidated house on the next corner that your children think is haunted.

What Do You Have in Common?

You may be asking yourself this very question. It is not easy to find an activity that will please your sixteen-year-old, your husband's eleven-year-old, and the two-year-old you have together. Being in a stepfamily requires a sense of adventure. Try out the kids' suggestions. Even if you hate the record your stepdaughter insists on having the family listen to, you have shared a common experience.

Differences and diversity abound in the stepfamily. You cannot expect the kind of identity the nuclear family next door seems to have. Your family events must go on even if one child is absent on a trip to another household. You cannot always wait until you are all together to have family times. An appreciation for those differences can become part of your family's identity.

Humor

Your sense of humor is one of your best tools for survival in your stepfamily. There must be times when your family would make a good situation comedy. When you can step back and put yourself in the role of an audience at these times, your stress will decrease, you will be able to laugh at yourself, and your humor can be shared with others.

Finally, take a modern outlook. Your family is pioneering a new life-style. You are proving that you don't have to be a biological parent to be loving, and you certainly don't have to be a biological parent to put your foot down. A new trend among first-married couples is to hyphenate their names. Your family is also hyphenated. Being proud of your new family and appreciating your spouse's efforts can give you a sense of a new identity as a person, as a couple, and as a family.

The Family in the Plain Brown Wrapper
Donna Bilbrey

We sat quietly and carefully, waiting for the photographer to take the last shots of our family portrait. Our smiles were feeling strangely taut and phony.

"It's amazing!" remarked the photographer. "One of your sons looks exactly like his father, and the other looks just like his mom." Genuine smiles flashed from all of us now. It was not so amazing that one of my sons had dark hair and eyes much like my own, and the other was blond and blue-eyed just like his dad. The towheaded little boy was my stepson, who had a blond, blue-eyed mom across town. The dark-haired little boy has a dark-haired dad somewhere in California. We all simply smiled at the young photographer's comment. We had been in this position many times before.

You just don't discuss your children's family trees with everyone. To the grocery clerk, the barber, and the car salesman, we appear quite the traditional family. To explain to passers-by who are the stepchildren, who are the natural ones, and how many marriages and divorces you and your present spouse have lived through is time-consuming and too personal. So as a blended family you sometimes feel as if you're enclosed in a plain brown wrapper.

The children seem to handle explanations much better than we adults: "Oh, he's not my *real* brother." But they can get more complicated, too. Since the birth of a third child and my husband's adoption of my son, my children have been heard to say, "Oh, yeah, well, Anthony is my half brother, and Robbie is my full brother. Anthony has a new stepbrother and stepsister since his real mom got married again. But my mom is still Anthony's stepmother." Whew!

No wonder we adults decline to explain our stepfamilies. But perhaps the reluctance goes even deeper. Perhaps it is a hesitation about laying open your past failures to near-strangers. I have not yet reached a point where I can say I am truly unashamed of having been married three times. My two divorces mark real failures for me and bring back old hurts and memories. Even though these divorces would be worth repeating for the love and friendship I have with my third husband, I am not eager to explain our blended family to most people.

I think the children's openness can teach us a simple lesson: remarriage and the resulting blended families need not be sealed for privacy in plain brown wrappers. I am not suggesting that we shout to the world how many times we've been married. But neither do we have to feel our past is tainted.

Every remarriage demonstrates two people's belief in the institution of marriage. We are not seeing the demise of the family in America, but its reorganization. Remarriage doesn't make you a loser; it makes you a winner. The losers are those people who have let one bad experience stop them from trying again.

"Where Do We Go from Here?"
Donna Bilbrey

Jack and Christie stand quietly before the justice of the peace. Today they begin their life together as man and wife. Behind them are Jack, Jr., age twelve, and Sandra, nine. To Christie's right is

Jason, six. He is clutching his mother's hand, trying hard to understand what is taking place. He does not quite grasp why his sister Veronica, ten, has refused to attend her mother's wedding. Instead, she has chosen to spend the weekend with her father.

When Jack and Christie step down from the altar today, their first question should be, "Where do we go from here?" Most remarried couples, however, do not ask this question. They come to their new union with the fantasy of becoming one big, happy family. Even if they have heard about the problems of living *in-step* from friends and family, they may ignore the early warning signs, such as a child's refusal to attend the wedding. Too many stepfamilies do not know how to deal effectively with the host of problems they soon will confront.

Professional counseling is recommended strongly for two families about to blend into one. Every stepfamily at one time or another will require this help. An estimated 95 percent do not seek it, however, even in the course of a serious crisis.

In beginning the process of blending two families, it is helpful to dispel common myths that often make the process that much more difficult. Be alert to the following myths and work at preventing them from taking hold.

Myth #1: Instant Love

The first and most prominent myth is thinking you will feel instant love for your spouse's children. You adore your new partner, so loving his or her children will come naturally . . . right? *Wrong!* They may be your spouse's children, but they also belong to someone else. These children will serve as a constant reminder of a previous intimate relationship. Although some stepparents will tell you loving their stepchildren presents no problem for them, many more honest stepparents will admit to having mixed feelings about the new family. It is not unusual to have deep, caring feelings for a stepchild, while still experiencing twinges of resentment.

Instant love can be a problem for children, too. In a new family, children particularly feel a sense of displacement and uncertainty about their position in the newly formed unit. Some kids, like Veronica, openly resist the formation of the stepfamily. Loyalty to the natural parent is the strongest factor in this resistance. It is important that this child be given space and allowed to adjust to new relationships at his or her own pace. Children should not be pushed into forming immediate relationships with stepparents or stepsiblings.

Myth #2: Equal Love

How many times have you heard stepparents profess they love their stepchildren just the same as their natural children. Any suggestion to the contrary may be taken as a personal insult.

The fact is, there is a difference in how one experiences love when the biological tie is absent. Not acknowledging this difference has been the downfall of many a blended family. Accepting this reality is a step in the right direction. A parent and child in a step relationship can have a genuinely deep affection for each other. It is possible, it is encouraged, but it is different from the feelings parents have for their natural children.

Myth #3: Children Come First

Sometimes the most damaging myth in a blended family is that the new couple must put the children first. In a second marriage, there is no *childless time*. You have an instant family, each member with values and personality already formed. The new couple's relationship must be the primary one. If husband and wife are committed to each other first, the rest will fall into place more easily. Children have an uncanny ability to spot a weak relationship, and they can surely destroy it.

A man and wife standing together in a united front can handle many assaults. Both spouses must put their past marriages behind them, legally and emotionally. Problems should be discussed openly and dealt with realistically. Also, both spouses must accept each other's children, but not let any child drive a wedge between them. Most important, both spouses must accept that they are not a biological family and do not react as such. They are a blended family.

Jack and Christie—along with Jack, Jr., Sandra, Jason, and Veronica—can have a rewarding life together as long as they continue to ask, "Where do we go from here?"

Can a Social Contract Help Integrate a Stepfamily?
Marie Kargman

Every family, whether it is a first-marriage family or a remarriage family, is a small, self-contained unit of government. Family members usually don't sit down and write a formal constitution, nor do they have legislative sessions. But when one member of the family feels a right has been infringed on or an obligation has not been met, there is conflict to resolve. Over time, family members learn the rights and obligations in their family.

The remarried family takes longer to make its own rules because each member of the remarried family is already imprinted with expectations from a previous family life. It may take years in the remarried family to sort out expectations learned in that previous family life from expectations in the present, reconstituted family. Family researchers, however, have recognized a cycle in stepfamily living that moves from the separateness of "mine" and "yours" into the cohesiveness of "ours." How can we assist this process of integration?

I think a premarital contract between families would help many stepfamilies achieve integration faster. We are all familiar with the concept of a business *merger*. No two businesses would consider merging without the help of a well-thought-out contract. Representatives of the merging businesses plus their advisers—lawyers, accountants, and the like—participate to identify all the differences in advance. Then they decide whether a harmonious merging can take place.

Each family is, for purposes of merging, a business. The members must learn to share living space, family income, family obligations, family time, and family affection. Family members have an investment in each other over time. When a previous marriage is dissolved, that family still continues as an economic and a business unit. Child support, alimony, or property from the former marriage evidence the business qualities that must be integrated into the remarriage.

The question is: How can a premarital contract move stepfamily integration along more quickly? A contract acknowledges the merging of two families. Both families, depending on the ages of the children, have the opportunity to explore and recommend what will be the power system or rules and regulations of this new unit. For example, teenagers might ask about using the family car.

The new stepfamily also will have its own family business: How will living space, affection, time, and money be shared? Will there be conflict between the old and the new? All the intimacies of the old family life should be discussed. What patterns of behavior already instilled will be changed now? If some of the children are married and have children or are divorced with children, will these grandchildren come for extended visits?

Therapists and counselors can help the members of two families planning on becoming one to understand and verbalize their attitudes, hopes, wishes, and fantasies. Disappointed expectations are an obstacle to a healthy stepfamily life. Getting expectations out in the open and evaluating them is beneficial to the two families who will live as one.

Will such a contract be enforceable in a court of law? The law does not recognize contracts between families, only between individuals who have the legal right to contract. So what good is the contract?

The premarital stepfamily contract is a social contract. Its purpose is twofold: (1) to improve the social conditions of two families under the same roof, and (2) to help two families integrate into a new unit.

Each member of the remarried family can benefit from the making of a family contract. A family contract provides for an arranged meeting where family members can express their wishes in an environment that protects each one from the questioning and chastisement of their views. This atmosphere is a precondition of the contract meeting.

The model for the premarital stepfamily contract is a conciliation court agreement invented by the California Conciliation Courts. It is entirely different from the premarital contract made by a contracting bride and groom, which usually provides for what will happen in case of divorce or death.

The premarital stepfamily contracts is to help family members have a better family life by providing solutions in advance for expected trouble spots.

When Eight Is Enough

Neal A. Kuyper

I grew up in a Dutch farm family of seven boys and three girls. My father saw his sons as free help in milking the cows, feeding the pigs, cleaning out the hen house, and chopping the wood for the ever-hungry stoves. My mother saw the girls as needed hands to help with endless cooking, jar upon jar of canning, sewing dresses, and keeping some order in the house. Going to school was incidental to the work that needed to be done for the survival of the family.

When my remarriage took place, it also created a large family, but without the survival anxiety of that early farm family. When my wife of twenty-four years died, I was left with four adolescents. The widow I married brought a teenage son and daughter to the new marriage. Suddenly we became a household of eight people, all virtual adults. Before we were married, this new marriage looked easy. There were five bedrooms in the house, and I had a study. I would give up my coveted study; two of the girls could share one bedroom, and all would be well. But after all was said and done, it didn't quite work that way.

It was fun planning for the wedding. My son and daughter became the best man and maid of honor, and my bride's son lit the candles. All the children, neighbors, and friends celebrated our new union at our chapel wedding.

Since the motel I had reserved for our wedding night had sent a postcard confirmation, the kids read it when picking up the mail. On the afternoon of the wedding, they decorated our room: balloons filled the bathroom, the bed was short-sheeted, and a boquet of flowers stood on the desk with these words: "We love you both. Have a wonderful honeymoon." It brought tears to our eyes, and we were thrilled. We had a new family, a large family.

But our family did not blend automatically. It needed some of the same cooperation I had experienced on the Minnesota farm. The children had their own life-style, which included basketball at school, Scouts every week, and piano lessons. They also had the idea that once Christina and I married, they were home free—relieved of all household duties. They envisioned Christina cooking and cleaning the house and me working to keep food on the table and gas in the car. They wanted healthy allowances and underwriting of the expenses that came with their extracurricular activities.

Once our three-day honeymoon was over, the family honeymoon was soon over, too. My youngest daughter resented losing half her room. My two boys felt my wife's son ought to mow the lawn, so it didn't get mowed at all. My oldest daughter and her son were certain they had been demoted in the family structure and resisted it. Freedom with the refrigerator had to be limited, so some food would be left for dinner.

Further irritations erupted when Christina griped about the lack of cooperation from my kids. In turn, I picked on hers. Lying in bed one night, we thought of getting a divorce to rear our children separately. The fun of our home was disappearing. The next night, we called the entire family around the kitchen table for "family time," and I made my speech: "We have had all the hell we are going to have in this household. Quit undermining the marriage! Let me assure you we are going to stay married, and you kids are going to cooperate."

My speech opened the floodgates of anger. The new marriage had caused too many changes for the children. When it all came out, Christina and I knew we had not prepared the children for blending into one household. It was a major life change for them to have a new mother and father, eight around the table, competition for the bathrooms, new restrictions on their freedom, and less attention from their parent.

We had to set up some structure in order to live together. We adjusted the allowances to the children's ages. We made a list of household chores such as setting the table, washing the dishes, mowing the lawn, and cleaning the house. Each had to give his or her room a good cleaning once a week. Mother would do the laundry, but each child would do his or her own ironing.

We set a limit on what we would pay toward clothing. If they wanted a more expensive item, they could pay the extra. I paid the standard rate for haircuts; they had to pay the extra for the fancy shop. Each paid five cents a mile for the use of the car. (Only after the children had left home did I realize they disconnected the speedometer half the time!)

Graduations began, from high school and then college. We determined how much we could contribute toward college educations; the children would have to earn the rest or obtain student loans. One of my daughters decided to attend a private, church-related college that was more expensive. We gave her the amount her education would have cost at the state school. When she went on for her master's degree, we loaned her part of the money, interest-free.

We established a set amount of money we could spend for each birthday, graduation, and Christmas. It has been difficult to stick to this when it comes to weddings. Each one is different, and inflation increases the costs. The arrival of grandchildren forced us to establish spending limits in this area, too.

In all this confusion, we have grown to love each other. Birthdays and holidays are very special. When the whole family is together, it is fun. They like to joke about times past. We try to help each other with moving, sharing plants for the garden, and being supportive of each other's careers. Listening to the children talk about their work, their leadership in the church, their travels adds luster to our days.

But the bonding was difficult, and much of the difficulty was related to lack of money, space, and time. I believe, however, that the lives of all six children are richer because of the remarriage. After the loss of a parent, they had the love of both a father and a mother again. They learned to make room for others and to appreciate differences. Blending two families has given our children a maturity that is reflected in their own life-styles. There is no doubt that we love each other and would fight for each other if necessary.

On Father's Day, all the children in the area come with their families and clean our yard as their gift to me. (It was my suggestion.) On Mother's Day we have a brunch at one of their homes. At least once a week, everyone calls to see how life is going for Christina and me. I am delighted that we had a *large family*, and a family that now increases each year. We love each one of them, and we feel their love for us.

Insights into Establishing
the Remarried Household

Claire Berman

"Two years ago I married a man with two daughters, ages eight and fourteen," said a young woman who wrote to me after an article I'd written about remarried families appeared in a popular national magazine. "It was a second marriage for both of us."

She went on: "My husband had given his wife a cash settlement and kept their home, which was filled with furniture, dishes, etc., that he and his first wife selected. I tried to imagine what problems might arise when we got married, but never once did I consider how much it would bother me to sit on a sofa my husband and his ex-wife picked out, serve guests on china that they chose, and then have my guests say, 'I love your dishes.'

"His wife had expensive tastes—only the best china, crystal, and silver would do—and I hate it. I told my husband I'd settle for stoneware, glass, and stainless steel, and help pay for it, but he thinks I'm being unreasonable. He just doesn't understand how important it is to make the house *our* home and not just *his.*"

The important questions of how to set up the remarried household, and where, should be addressed *before* the wedding ceremony takes place. These decisions center on more than matters of decor and location; they also have to do with history (the ghosts of the previous marriage often continue to lurk in rooms and hallways) and with territoriality. The parent and child or children who lived in the house before the remarriage tend to become the "home team," while the person or persons moving in are the "visitors."

The sensible move is not always the right one. It made sense, for example, for Sam to leave the cramped bachelor quarters he'd established following his separation from his first wife and move in with Helen and her family when he embarked on his second marriage. Helen's home was spacious, so her three children would not have to be uprooted from their rooms, and there was even a family room where Sam's children could stay when they visited. It made sense—except, as Sam describes it, "I always felt like an intruder."

It is difficult for someone who feels like an intruder to assert himself. In this home, Sam was a guest—one who was not welcomed by all the inhabitants. Nor did he feel free to make his own children welcome: he (and they) were too busy being careful not to scratch the coffee table or spill anything on the pale velvet rug. What did, in fact, make sense was for this remarried couple to establish a new home to accommodate their newly reorganized family.

But isn't that expensive? Generally, that's the first question couples will raise. And the answer is yes. But men and women who are concerned about the high cost of new housing often fail to realize that rising real estate values are also likely to bring a higher purchase price for any property they are selling. Similar reasoning applies even if neither of the partners owns a home. If each has lived in an apartment, chances are that the two rentals combined will cover the expense of a single mutual residence.

Where to establish a home for the new family is more than a dollars-and-cents decision. For Jeanne and Peter, their decision to reside in Jeanne's house was based on the fact that Jeanne wanted to disrupt her children's lives as little as possible. She wanted them to remain in their schools and retain their old friends. But the house did not work well for Peter, who chafed at his stepdaughter's frequent reminders that Daddy built the desk where Peter now sat, that Daddy planted the bushes Peter was pruning. Jeanne and Peter were much happier when they exchanged this house for another in the same community.

That solution did not work for Mary Ann and Dave, who found that a move to a different community was called for. In the small town where Dave and his ex-spouse both continued to live after their divorce, Dave's new wife, Mary Ann, found herself running into her predecessor at the hairdresser, the supermarket, the church social. Some distance clearly was necessary—and a move to a nearby community (different church and beauty salon) provided the answer.

Where to live is an emotional as well as a practical decision. It deserves careful thought—*especially* by men and women who are striving to create a harmonious environment the second time around.

Buying a *New* Home for a *New* Family

Neal A. Kuyper

For one year Christina and I lived in the house where my first wife and I had lived. With her two teenagers and my four of the same age, we tried to make this house *our* home. But the influence of my first marriage was present in color combinations of the walls, drapes, and rugs. Christina's furniture was wedged in among mine. The result: Christina's children felt like visitors in our new blended family.

I resisted every hint that we should move to a different house. We already had three bathrooms for eight people. I was paying a low interest rate of 5.8 percent on the decreasing mortgage. Where could I find this again? The neighbors were my friends, even if they did not accept my new wife. My four children were settled in school. They already had adjusted to their mother's death and a new marriage. Finally, however, it became clear to me that we would be a divided family until we moved into a new house.

It was the best move we ever made. Christina and I sorted out items we no longer needed in the new home. Those belonging to my first marriage were placed on the recreation room floor for my children to divide among themselves for future use. Silverware, dishes, kitchenware, tablecloths all found their way into separate boxes to be stored for the day when the children established their own homes. Next we had a big garage sale to siphon more excess goods. The Salvation Army picked up the leftovers, and we were ready to move.

In the new house everything blended together—no more of this is mine and this is yours. We became a family. With new neighbors, new friends, a new school, and a new community, we all shared alike in starting over as a family.

If one or both of you own a home now, there are many things to consider in purchasing a new one. Here are some of the options:

Sell both homes and reinvest in a new home.

Keep one or both homes for income.

Move together into one of the homes.

Keep one home to rent to the children.

You'll also want to think about some other considerations:

Schools. If your children are of school age, is it a good time to move? If a teenager is a high school senior, you may want to wait until after graduation. Sometimes the child can commute to school for that year. Most children adjust to a new school when they have helped plan for the move.

Location. Have you wanted to move to the inner city, the suburbs, the country, or a condominium? Perhaps now is the right time to consider another part of the United States, even another country. Is this the place you will want to spend your retirement years?

Extras. What about more closet space? Now you can look for a garage with a workbench, a fenced yard for your dog, or no yard at all. Have you always wanted a fireplace, a den, a sewing room, a guest room, walk-in closets, a plant window in the kitchen? Some of these can be realities in your new home.

Transportation. Do you want to be closer to work? Accessibility of a bus line, a train, or a freeway may be an important factor in choosing the location of the new home.

Type of home. Are you interested in buying an old home and repairing it? Some spend hours mulling over plans and design their own new home. House hunting is tedious, but it helps clarify the type of home you want as well as price range you can afford.

Some of the advantages of buying a new home are:

Starting over in a place that has no history with a former spouse

Blending furnishings and ridding yourselves of unnecessary items

Obtaining many features you may want in a home in your maturing years

Making a long-term investment that gives stability to the new marriage

Some of the possible complications are:

An unwillingness to change your environment and sell the old house

Fear of closing costs, higher interest rates, a larger mortgage, increased taxes, and more indebtedness

Determining payable taxes or exemptions

Children's resistance to moving to a new neighborhood, leaving behind friends and a familiar school

Inadequate funds to buy a new home

Buying a new home in a remarriage may be a frightening risk. It also can be an exciting adventure.

Dealing with Discipline
Elizabeth Einstein

In first families, sex and money are the big troublemakers. In remarriages, however, most problems center on the children. To make stepfamily living more successful, the greatest hurdle couples need to conquer is dealing with discipline.

The ideal time to start making a mutual plan for rearing the children is during courtship. Warnings of problem areas are usually there if couples pay attention. Watching how your partner deals with his or her youngsters' misbehaviors may reveal diverse approaches to discipline and raise serious questions about how the children will be reared. The best investment a remarried couple—or, better yet, a couple approaching remarriage—can make is to enroll in a parenting class. In this supportive environment, adults can gain new skills and sensitivities to each other's style of parenting.

When couples can develop a compatible style of disciplining the children, this *united front* provides security for the children and makes for swifter decisions regarding discipline. A united front does not mean that both adults must agree on everything, but they do need to support each other's decisions. It is important that parents and stepparents be aware of their individual approaches to discipline. Their way may not be as effective as they would wish and — unaware of other options — they may simply be doing what they learned from their own parents.

Most parents use one of three basic discipline styles: *authoritarian, permissive,* or *democratic.* Some adults use the "boss" approach to discipline — yelling, commanding, ordering, rewarding, bribing, and punishing; their children may obey from fear but develop little self-control or self-esteem. Permissive parents plead, cajole, and wish for their children to behave, but fail to set boundaries or consequences for misbehavior. Youngsters brought up under this approach become self-centered and have little self-control.

The ideal approach to discipline is the democratic style, where parents and children share the power in a home atmosphere that is relaxed and consistent. Children are encouraged to think, contribute, and cooperate; parents are approachable, reasonable, and respected. Relationships between parents and children are open and respectful; they share and communicate with one another. The discipline tools for adults using the democratic parenting style include incentives, setting consequences for misbehavior, negotiation, requesting, and conflict resolution.

The democratic approach to discipline is wise for all families because of the warm home atmosphere it creates and its ultimate benefits for the children. For stepfamilies trying to stabilize themselves, this discipline approach is especially important because it creates cooperation and helps build bonds — two essential elements as two families attempt to merge their diverse ways into what works for the new stepfamily.

Discipline is a form of love. All children need rules, limits, and boundaries in order to feel their parents love them. Stepchildren (who have experienced much loss and many transitions) especially need to know that the adults rearing them care enough to set both limits and consequences for their misbehavior, when they test those limits.

What role does a stepparent play in discipline? Should stepparents be involved in disciplining stepchildren at all? Eventually, yes. But as the new stepfamily is forming, it is wise for new stepparents to leave the task of discipline to the biological parent. Waiting to become involved in any disciplinary action gives the stepparent time to be included in the children's thinking. It also leaves time for trust and respect to develop—the necessary base from which discipline works.

The temptation to involve stepparents in discipline too soon may come from a spouse who feels ineffectual in getting the children to behave. One unconscious motive for remarriage may be to seek a spouse who will be a savior in straightening out the kids. This doesn't work. When stepparents jump in as disciplinarians, whether encouraged by the spouse or not, problems usually get worse.

As relationships grow and stepparents begin to take a part in discipline, children still may resist. Often resistance means the new stepparent is being tested. Other reasons for resistance may include resentment at the intrusion, lack of trust or confidence that the new family will work, and displaced anger at the missing biological parent.

Taking time to become involved in disciplining stepchildren also provides continuity for the children. During single-parent living, children become used to a particular discipline style, effective or not. This approach may be quite different from the style the new stepparent uses or thinks should be used. But when stepparents try to make changes or take over as disciplinarians in these critical, early stages of stepfamily development, the attempts are bound to create trouble, especially between stepparent and stepchildren and between the new marriage partners.

To summarize, until time and developing relationships make disciplining possible, it is wise to let the biological parent take care of the discipline, for these reasons:

Youngsters are used to a certain kind of discipline from their parents. With so many other changes happening in their lives, consistency in this area is important.

Waiting to discipline stepchildren gives youngsters time to build a stronger relationship with their stepparent first.

The stepparent is not forced into the role of the *heavy* and can remain in a more neutral position.

The new couple have time to merge their diverse approaches to parenting and disciplining by either talking them through or taking parenting classes.

When stepparents are left alone with stepchildren, they may have to deal with misbehavior immediately. Waiting until Dad gets home is ineffective in any family. To cover this possibility, biological parents must transfer their authority to discipline to stepparents, in front of the children. Your spouse can simply say, "When I'm not home, Jane and I have agreed to . . ." This lets the children know you are working together and in their best interests. When they test you—and most likely they will—your spouse will support you because you have planned your strategy together in advance.

When your children see you working together as a team, they will begin to feel more secure. With this security, your stepfamily can stabilize itself and work toward success.

Helping Remarried Families Deal with Weekend Children
Joan Weiss

At a recent stepfamily meeting, Carla, a stepmother, talked of the coming and going of children on weekends, and how uncomfortable they made her. During the week, Carla and her husband Tim live with Carla's two sons, ten-year-old Ron and eight-year-old Peter, and with Tim's oldest daughter Shelly, age twelve. Ron and Peter spend every weekend with their father, and three weekends a month Shelley is away with her mother. Tim's other two daughters, Franny and Paula, ages nine and seven, come every other weekend.

Such complex arrangements are not unusual in stepfamilies. In Carla and Tim's family, there are sometimes five children at home, sometimes two, rarely none. Working out a month in advance who will be home for a particular weekend is an intellectual challenge. Carla told the group, "I don't know who is in my family and who is not." In nuclear families this complaint would never arise, because children don't shuttle like boxcars between stations.

When children go back and forth between two households, causing families to expand and contract from week to week or even day to day, both adults and children feel confused as well as overwhelmed at times. Carla's son Peter is the oldest child when his stepsister leaves for the weekend, but not after she returns. Franny and Paula wonder what they should call Carla's mother when she visits, *Grandma* or *Mrs. Smith*. Sometimes children have their own bedrooms, sometimes not. Some days there is more competition for a parent's attention than on other days.

Stepparents and parents need to talk about these tensions created by weekend visits. At another stepfamily meeting, a major issue was raised by Anne whose stepson visits two weekends a month. She asked: "If kids don't live with you most of the time, should you treat them like guests when they visit? Is it easier to stretch the rules and hold your breath until Sunday evening or to say, 'On weekends you live with us and are a member of this household. This is how things are done in this household.'"

Most stepparents say, "Yes, treat the child like a member of the family, not like a guest." Telling a child that he or she "lives with us" for weekends redefines the child's place in the family, making it less special and providing a sense of normality.

Sometimes noncustodial fathers allow their weekend children to act up and escape rules because they fear their children will not visit if disciplined. Noncustodial fathers also try to squeeze in all the special treats and good times they cannot provide when the children are at home with their mothers. This indulgence is unlikely to sit well with a stepmother who sees one set of rules for her kids and another set for the visiting child.

For stepmothers without children of their own, weekend visits also present problems. Renee, a stepmother of six months, says: "I really find Tim a delightful, bright, wonderful six-year-old. I used to teach school and looked forward to being his stepmother. But seeing him every weekend and having Bob tense all week in anticipation of the visit, and then collapse into a depressed state Sunday night when Tim leaves is taking its toll on me and the relationship."

Weekends are difficult for the visiting child as well as the entire family. The visiting child may resent having to follow a schedule instead of being free like other kids on weekends. It can also be upsetting to see Dad living in another home with another set of kids and a new wife. It can feel unfair sleeping on a sofa-bed or an army cot in a strange room, when her kids have beds and rooms of their own.

If the stepfather hears complaints, he is apt to feel unjustly accused. He is doing his best, yet he is unappreciated. One stepfather said: "I live with Laura's kids all the time. I feel that when my children come over, Laura's kids shouldn't gripe about having to double up."

There is no magic remedy for the dislocations and hurt feelings that visiting causes. These feelings are manageable, however, when people are open about their emotions, respectful of each other, and committed to making their stepfamily work.

Many stepfamilies find family meetings valuable because everyone has a chance to speak up. It is also important for the two parents to present themselves clearly as partners, who consult with each other about the family's management and support each other in their daily lives. Openness, mutual respect, structure, and flexibility are useful to any family. For a remarried family, they are essential.

Helpful Hints for Weekend Visits

Give the visiting child a permanent place such as a drawer, shelf, or closet to keep his or her things. Also make sure things are left behind: a toothbrush, comb, or books.

Establish consistent routines to follow or chores to do during visits. Assign the child a place at the dinner table, so it won't be musical chairs when he or she comes for the weekend.

Don't overdo special activities. Let a natural, relaxing environment evolve for the entire family.

Spend time alone with each child in the family.

Encourage the child to bring a friend for the weekend.

Use family meetings to get children involved in the workings of the households.

Attempting to Reconcile
Conflicting Interests in a Stepfamily
Robert S. Weiss

A while ago a couple came to see me. He was a professional man, quiet and pleasant, but obviously worried. She too was a professional (in another field), solicitous of her husband but possibly a bit critical as well. The problem was the man's former wife, who, the man said, was invasive, insensitive, and disruptive. What could they do about her?

The man had one child by his first marriage, a boy, now fourteen years old. The boy had been four when the man's marriage ended. For the next six years, four times a year, the man visited his son, flying to the part of the country where his wife had moved. Each summer the boy spent a month with him.

Two years ago, when the boy was twelve, his father remarried. Not long after, his former wife also remarried and, with her new husband, returned to her ex-husband's part of the country.

At this point the boy decided he wanted to live with his father and new stepmother. He explained that he wanted to get to know his father before his childhood ended. The man was pleased, and his new wife accepted this arrangement, although it wasn't what she had planned on.

The first wife seemed to go along with the boy's plan. She phoned him regularly—every evening, in fact. Whenever the spirit moved her, she would drive to her ex-husband's house to talk with their son, look at his homework, invite him out for supper. Once the man's new wife came home to find the former wife in their front room reading a book, waiting for their son to return from school. The new wife thought that was a bit much.

The man had asked his former wife to call before coming over, and not to call so often. His former wife argued that she was their son's mother. Didn't she have the right to be in touch with him?

This is a particularly vivid instance of a common conflict in stepfamily homes. Children, noncustodial parents, custodial parents, and stepparents have conflicting desires. What each wants is inconsistent with what the others want.

Children want easy access to both their parents; they want their parents to remain in their world. Noncustodial parents want access to their children, without barriers. Custodial parents want their children's needs to be met; they want to be good parents-in-charge. Stepparents want to meet their responsibilities to their stepchildren, but they also want to protect the integrity of their homes and marriages.

How might this family reconcile their potentially conflicting interests? Just recognizing them and acknowledging that everyone has a right to achieve his or her goals is a beginning. The next step is to realize that the goals of those involved are truly in conflict, and that if just one person achieves everything he or she wants, this will impose penalties on the others. The final step is to try to work out a system that gives everyone what is essential to him or her, even though it means everyone also has to give something up.

Essential to the stepmother is that she feel secure within the boundaries of her home and her marriage. The former wife will have to ask the stepmother's permission before entering her home and will have to cut down on phone calls to the son. The boy will have to discuss with his stepmother when he wants to invite his mother in. The man will have to be on his new wife's side if she feels herself invaded again.

Essential to the boy is easy access to his mother as well as to his father. He should know that he can see his mother—in *her* home—whenever he wants, but he has to let his father or stepmother know where he is. He should know he can call his mother at any time.

Essential to the first wife is easy access to her son. She should know that calls from her will be welcomed on particular evenings, but not on other evenings. It can create a problem in the home if she ties up the family phone.

Essential to the man is that it all works. He should assume responsibility for acting if someone complains. Everyone should acknowledge that he is the one to approach with complaints. The father is responsible for trying to set matters right.

Did this solve the problem? I think it improved matters, although I really can't be sure. Reconciling conflicting interests is not an attempt to set things right once and for all. Rather, it recognizes the different aims and investments of the people involved and attempts to set in motion a system that—given patience and mutual understanding among those involved—can respond with some effectiveness to the new difficulties that will inevitably occur.

How to Deal with Sexual Feelings in the Stepfamily
Claire Berman

Stepfamilies often include members who are not biologically connected, who may in fact be virtual strangers to one another, but who are expected to live together in an intimate family setting. It is no wonder that this unit is likely to be highly sexually charged.

To begin with, husband and wife are newlyweds. Thus the atmosphere in the home is more affectionate and romantic than in first-wed families (by the time the children arrive). Unlike those youngsters whose reaction upon being told the facts of life is, "Not *my* parents," children in stepfamilies are very much aware that the remarried couple is sexually active. Some may resent this, seeing it as inappropriate for people *that* age or as a betrayal of their other parent. Others will be intrigued and find their own sexual feelings aroused.

The remarried couple should be aware of these feelings and try to confine their romantic behavior to the bedroom. This is not to suggest that the couple ought to behave as platonic friends. Romantic signs are honest expressions of their affection. What's more, it is good for children—especially for those who have witnessed a hostile and divisive relationship between the parents in their first home—to see the remarried parent valued and a healthy, loving relationship expressed. Moderation (not abstinence) is a reasonable guideline for the public behavior of husband and wife in the new union.

Other sexual issues may be more difficult to manage. These include sexual feelings between stepparent and stepchild or between stepsiblings. We are talking about feelings here, not actions, and those who live in stepfamilies would do well to acknowledge, first, that such feelings exist.

The stepfather, for example, may see in his stepdaughter a

younger, firm-bodied version of the woman he fell in love with. It is not surprising for there to be some electricity in the air: an adolescent daughter, growing into her own womanhood, extends the competition with her mother by flirting with her mother's new husband. (Similar feelings and actions take place between stepmother and stepson.) The biological barrier does not exist—husband and stepdaughter, wife and stepson are *not* genetically related. The psychological barrier, however, must be respected. It is the adult's job to be aware of the possibility of sexual feelings at play in the remarried family, and to see to it that sexual fantasies are not acted out.

A biological parent who suspects that inappropriate behavior is taking place has a duty to intercede. One woman noticed that her teenage daughter had taken to parading around the house in a bikini and spending inordinate amounts of time sunbathing in the backyard, especially when her stepfather was at home. She called her husband's attention to what was going on, made him recognize that his stepdaughter was flirting with him and face the fact that he was flattered and was encouraging the young girl's attentions. The woman then told her daughter that a stricter dress code was now in force. This family reports that once the rules were understood, the atmosphere in the home became more relaxed and relationships among family members improved.

Sexual stirrings are also common between stepsiblings who are brought together for short or longer periods. Sometimes the attraction may be well disguised. "I hate him," one teenager may say of her stepbrother when, in fact, that "hatred" may be a defense against growing feelings of caring. (On the other hand, she may indeed dislike him, for a variety of reasons. Sex need not be at the core of every emotional response!)

It is probably wise for parents who suspect that sexual attraction is an issue between their children to defuse the tension in the home by planning group activities (with a parent present) and trying not to leave the young people unattended in the home. If sexual feelings are acted upon—between adult and stepchild or between the children—professional help must be sought.

In most remarried households, sexual issues are managed along with the other stresses that go into building a family. They are cause for awareness, not alarm.

8

What Are the Children Feeling?

The Question of Children at the Wedding

Neal A. Kuyper

He wants the children at the wedding, and I don't want them present to see him marry that woman.

This is an irate former spouse's response to her ex-husband's request for the presence of his children at his wedding. She may have her reasons. If she still believed in a possibility of reconciliation, a remarriage closes the book. Or she may not have come to terms with the fact that someone else could love her husband, whom she found so unlovable. The children's glowing reports of their dad's new friend may have stirred up a bit of jealousy. Whatever the reason, the former wife resists allowing the children at the wedding.

In my work as a pastoral counselor, I have performed many remarriages, and I always encourage the presence of the children at the wedding. They need to experience this new beginning for their parent. It fixes in their mind that this "new mom" or this "new dad" is a reality. They now know that their natural parents will not reconcile. As a new family is being formed, they witness it coming into being with all the honor and dignity of a wedding. They can join with family and friends to celebrate this milestone of change.

Even grandchildren have been present at such weddings. A sixty-six-year-old widower and his bride of equal years had their whole family present. She wanted to come down the aisle in a flowing dress. Many years ago she had been married in North Dakota in the parson's home. This time she wanted to fulfill her dreams with a church wedding. The grandchildren sprinkled rose petals down the aisle as she went to the altar on the arm of her son. A brother and sister stood with the couple as witnesses. Grandchildren ushered, poured at the reception, prepared many of the refreshments. It was a true family celebration. At the close of the wedding we asked all the children and grandchildren to come into the chancel for the closing prayer. We joined hands three deep around the couple. As the newlyweds started down the aisle after the benediction, the audience applauded.

Some of the most interesting weddings have taken place in the home of the couple or a member of the family. Children love to take part in these weddings. One son played the flute as a prelude to the wedding. In a Jewish wedding where both persons had been divorced, they set up the traditional canopy. The father of the groom addressed the couple on love and marriage. The husband's two boys and the wife's daughter spent the time wide-eyed, watching the events and making sneak attacks on the goodies colorfully displayed on the table. They too took part in the ceremony and held hands as a new family in the closing prayers. When my wife and I married—she a widow and I a widower—we had all six children take part in the wedding.

It is equally important to have other family members and friends at a reception. One couple were married by a justice of the peace and then took off immediately for a honeymoon in Hawaii. Their children were confused by their sudden disappearance, and the new bride later confided to me that she had never really felt married. When he resisted having any reception, it was as if her husband were ashamed of her. I suggested that the only solution was to invite family and friends to an *open house reception* at their home. In this case, the basic problem was this man had not let go emotionally of his deceased wife.

In response to a former spouse's resistance to having the children at the wedding, I would think about some of the following:

1. For children who have experienced the painful end of a marriage by death or divorce, it is reassuring to know that their parent

can love again and rebuild a life with another person. It is a way of moving from despair to hope.

2. The new stepparent will be sharing the bed in the master bedroom. They know this is all right because they have seen the couple married.

3. Children love weddings. Wedding preparations are fun. Dressing up at the appointed hour means a special occasion. Taking part in the wedding or the reception feels like helping Dad or Mom get married. Listening to the words of the ceremony and the vows helps children realize the seriousness of this decision to marry.

4. It is important for the children to be acknowledged in the wedding ceremony. This acknowledgment can be stating their names or asking the children to be present at the closing prayer of blessing or at the reading of a scripture. Perhaps a child could play a musical instrument or sing a solo. At one wedding, we prearranged with the children to respond to the question, "Who gives this woman to be married to this man?" The children responded, "We do"—a pleasant surprise for the parents.

5. When the children are present at the reception, they meet members of the stepparent's family and friends as well as members of their own family. This affirmation of a community of persons adds to the *rightness* of this new union.

6. When the parent and the stepparent return from the honeymoon (if any), it marks the official beginning of the formation of this new family. The children have witnessed the commitment these two adults (their parents) have made to each other in marriage, which should stop further attempts to bring their natural parents back together. The wedding ceremony is a good beginning for the bonding process with the stepparent.

"Is It All Right to Love My Stepparent?"
Joan Weiss

Children in remarried families are often caught in situations of divided loyalties. For example, Amanda's father has recently married Jane. Jane, who is childless, and eight-year-old Amanda are getting to know each other. They decide on a day at the beach with Dad.

Jane makes Amanda's favorite sandwiches, Dad is delighted to spend time with his daugther, and Amanda has been looking forward to the outing all week. Initially, all goes well. Then Amanda's mood changes. She becomes withdrawn and cranky. Jane feels hurt and puzzled, wondering if she has said or done something to upset Amanda. In fact, she has. Jane has been *too* nice. Amanda found herself liking her stepmother so much that she began to feel she was betraying her mother.

When a parent remarries, children are faced with complex feelings to sort out in choosing where to place their affections. The conflict can express itself like this: "Jane seems really nice, but if I like her, Mom will be hurt. And how come it has to be Dad and Jane? How come it's not Dad and Mom?"

One mother realized her daughter's emotional dilemma when she kept describing her visits with her father and stepmother in negative terms. This mother sensitively recognized that her child felt it was disloyal to say anything positive about her stepmother. This mother said: "Darling, I know it makes you sad that Dad and I don't live together anymore. It sometimes makes me sad, too. But Dad and Beth are together now, and it's okay for you to talk about the nice things that happen. I won't feel hurt if you and Beth have good times together."

By giving a child permission to enjoy a relationship with a stepparent, you free the child to some degree from the loyalty bind. Not wanting to anger or to lose a parent's love, children will follow the parent's lead in establishing relationships. Children need to be reassured that having a warm relationship with a stepparent will not endanger the relationship with their biological parent.

Stepparents can help, too, by allowing children to talk about the biological parent. Talking may include stories about Mom and Dad together and some of the good times they had. Biological parents may feel that their children must never allude to anything positive in the previous marriage because it undercuts the reasons for divorce. In reality, however, there are good as well as bad memories in all marriages.

Children's loyalty conflicts can be more complex when a parent dies. The child may idealize the dead parent and be fiercely loyal to the memory. It is important to allow children to talk about the parent who has died, remembering him or her with human strengths and frailties. If the parent is never discussed, the child has only idealized memories. This makes it more difficult to become close to a stepparent.

Stepparents, especially stepmothers, who spend more time with the children, may view rejection as a personal affront, rather than seeing it as a loyalty struggle. One stepmother said: "It's a no-win situation. If I go out of my way to do something special for my stepson, it's not as good as something his mother did. If I play it cool, I'm in the wicked stepmother category."

Loyalty issues are made even worse when parents engaging in a hostile battle try to recruit the children as allies. A parent's anger is identified easily without verbalizing it. The way a mother tenses up when her child is on the phone with Dad, or the abruptness with which a support check is handed over, clearly communicates a parent's feelings. It is important for former spouses to control angry and heated interchanges when children are present.

Another tendency to guard against is making unfavorable comparisons between a former spouse and a new partner. "Your father never helped you with your homework the way Joe does." "Boy, it's great being married to someone who can cook." This approach is guaranteed to engender intense feelings of loyalty toward the absent parent.

We know that when children of divorced parents have a good, ongoing relationship with both biological parents, they are more likely to relax and develop a comfortable relationship with the stepparent. To ease the transition for children when a new friend or a stepparent is introduced into their lives, it is important to have a careful, honest discussion about what changes will be happening. You also should assure them of their continued place in the family and in your affection.

Surnames Cause Confusion
for Courts and Families

Marie Kargman

Two mothers, one in New Jersey and one in Illinois, fight for the right to change the surname of a child by a previous marriage to the mother's new surname.

After giving you the facts in both cases, I will discuss the decision in each case, what these decisions have in common, how they differ, and the implications of these decisions for remarried persons. (These cases are true, but the names have been changed.)

Case #1

In New Jersey, Betty Eisnor applies to the New Jersey Superior Court, Law Division, to change her son's name from Thomas Desmond to Thomas Eisnor. Eisnor was her maiden name, which she resumed after her divorce from Thomas's father, Joseph Desmond. Her son Thomas was born in 1981; the couple was divorced in 1982. Betty tells the court that since their separation the father has seen his son only twice: once for half an hour on Thomas's first birthday, and again for five minutes during Christmas 1982. Before the divorce, Joseph was rarely home and spent little time with his son.

Betty says that because her son is always with her, she believes he should share her name. She also suggests that if her son shares her name, it will be less awkward for him as he grows older.

The father opposes the name change in court. He says this decision to change his son's name is contrary to all previous decisions for changing of names in the state of New Jersey.

The judge admits his opinion disagrees with the leading cases in New Jersey, which state a father has "the right to have his kin to bear his name." For this reason, the judge writes his opinion—not the usual custom in lower court, where opinions are verbal. In his written opinion the judge says:

> The right of a father to have his child bear his name is no greater than
> the right of a mother to have a child bear her name . . . the deference

to the father is a deference rooted in antiquity. It echoes fortunately disappearing sexual values.

A child whose name is not changed may feel rejected by the mother's resumption of her maiden name (lost by marriage custom) or the mother's assumption of the surname of a new husband (acquired in order to provide a family setting for the child). Mother may be considered deserving of rejection/contempt for the failure to share her new name with her child.

Names, as this case clearly illustrates, are intimately involved with the status of women. Rules of law for changing names cannot be premised upon unacceptable theories of inequality. The right of a mother to have her child bear her name must be recognized as equal to that of the father. The sole consideration when parents contest a surname should be the child's best interest, tempered by extenuating circumstances.

Going beyond the facts in this case (but relevant to the case to be discussed next), the judge then quoted from a California case with which he agreed:

> The symbolic role that a surname other than the natural father's may play in easing relations with a new family should be balanced against the importance of maintaining the biological father–child relationship. The embarrassment or discomfort that a child may experience when he bears a surname different from the rest of the family should be evaluated.

In this case the name change was granted.

Case #2

In our next case, we will ask: "Did the judge consider the discomfort of Brad Parsons when he refused Brad the right to call himself by his mother's remarried name, which is Kiley?"

In Illinois, Andrea Kiley—formerly Andrea Parsons in her first marriage—is now happily remarried. Brad, her seven-year-old son, is living with her, her new husband, and his two children. Soon after Andrea's remarriage, Brad said he wanted the same last name as the rest of the family. "All right," said his mother, "we'll just call you Brad Kiley. Would you like that?" Brad was delighted. He asked his friends in school and on the playground to call him Kiley, just as they did his stepsiblings. To make it less confusing for Brad, his mother told the school they could change Brad's name on the school record. This permission was what would later cause her trouble.

Brad's father, angry about this informal name change, accused Andrea of changing Brad's name without his permission. When Andrea refused to order Brad to stop calling himself Kiley, Brad's father filed a petition in the divorce court that had originally given custody of Brad to his mother. He accused Andrea of violating the custody order. Andrea said: "What I call Brad and what others call Brad at his request is a personal matter. We are not trying to change Brad's name legally. We are calling him by the name he prefers." In support of her behavior, Andrea says: "Brad has the common-law right to call himself any name he wishes. Adults have this right—why not children?"

Brad's father asked the divorce court to forbid all persons from calling Brad by any other name than Brad Parsons. Andrea said the divorce court had no jurisdiction in a name dispute. The divorce court said it did have jurisdiction, because any dispute between divorced parents centering around a child is a custody dispute. Andrea and everyone else were forbidden to call Brad anything but Parsons. Andrea then appealed to a higher court.

Reviewing the decision of the lower court, the Illinois Supreme Court said it had never had a case like this before. The upper court addressed this question: Can the divorced father of a seven-year-old boy prevent the child from being called by the surname of his mother's new husband until the child is old enough to change his name legally?

Answering the question, the court wrote:

A de facto change accomplished by substituting Kiley for Parsons on Bradford's school, medical, and other records may have as great an effect on Bradford's daily life as a legal change. Since the court has jurisdiction to enjoin a legal change of name proceeding, it has jurisdiction to enjoin any other formal change of name as well. . . . A change in a minor's surname shall be allowed only when the court finds that the change is in the best interest of the minor child. . . . After his parents divorced and remarried, Brad's life could never be the same as those of his peers living in intact families. Since his mother's remarriage, he now has a different name than his mother and stepsiblings with whom he lives. This may cause some concern, confusion and embarrassment for him and for his mother, but that alone is not enough to warrant changing Brad's name. . . . The noncustodial parent necessarily is at a disadvantage in maintaining a strong relationship with the child and maintenance of that parent's name goes far toward demonstrating his continuing interest in and identity with the child. . . .

The lower-court order went too far, however, said the Illinois Supreme Court. It should not have extended the law to informal situations within the family:

There are some relationships which the law does not have the capacity to control—the name a child asks others to call him on the playground is one of them. It would be extremely difficult to enforce such an order. . . . Although we appreciate that the consistent use of a single name is important to the child's emotional development, we will not approve the entry of an order which the circuit court cannot enforce.

The Outcome

In New Jersey, the mother asked the court for permission to change the name of the child. In Illinois, the mother found herself in court against her will to defend her child's right to call himself by her new surname.

In New Jersey, the judge asked, "Where do children get their surnames? Does the child have the right to a mother's surname as well as to a father's surname?" In Illinois, the judge asked, "How can you expect a father to support a child if the child doesn't have his name?" Both courts held their decisions to be in the best interests of the child.

In New Jersey, the judge's personal philosophy of sexual discrimination in the naming of children is as much a part of the *facts* in this case as are the facts presented to the court by the parents. In Illinois, the lower court's sympathy for the noncustodial father, reflected in an order so broad that part of it had to be reversed as nonenforceable, was also a *fact* in the case.

Perhaps we need more information and discussion about changing the surnames of children in remarried families. The following quote, from a review of the book *Daddy's New Baby*, by Judith Vigna, reinforces the confusion that surrounds the issue of surnames in remarriage. A little girl, chatting about her baby half-sister, worries that people won't know they are sisters. She says, "A girl at school has a different last name than her new brother. Some of the teachers don't know they're from the same family."

Helping Older Children Adjust in a Blended Family

Neal A. Kuyper

In most cases, remarriage brings an instant package of children, from tiny, nursing infants to adolescents who resist their newly constituted family. It is far easier for young children to adapt to new mothers or fathers than it is for adolescents.

The adolescent has learned to live in his family through day-to-day events. Toilet habits, choice of foods, study expectations, use of television, required chores, and space for recreation have contributed to forming a structure for living in the household. The stepparent brings new expectations and changes, which can be upsetting. For example, the master bedroom suddenly becomes off limits, and bedtime comes earlier. Such changes can appear as an infringement on personal rights.

During the time the adolescent lived with only one of his parents, a special bonding took place because the parent's undivided attention was available. With a new parent on the horizon, the adolescent grieves the loss of this special bond instead of seeing the benefits of gaining another parent.

An invasion of space can take place with a new marriage, too. When George married Sharon, he brought with him his teenage daughter Julie. Sharon had two boys with separate rooms. With Julie there, the boys had to double up, and they resented the loss of their private space. In addition, Sharon set new limits on her sons' previous freedom to devour food in the refrigerator. The couch in front of the television even took on a new aura. It became the place where George and Sharon sat and held hands instead of the favorite place it had been for lying around and reading. Julie also found it difficult to adjust to this new home, where she had to contend with stepbrothers, a stepmother, and a new school.

Loyalty to the biological parent also creates stress for the adolescent. He or she can easily feel guilty about giving affection to a new parent. At the same time, this affection acknowledges there is no hope of the biological parents reuniting. Often, an adolescent will shout, in anger and pain, "I want to go back to my real mom or dad."

Adolescents often look upon kisses and hugs between the new partners as disloyalty to the natural parent. Most children have seen their parents as asexual. Now there is a new man or woman in their parent's bed. They know the couple are sexual behind the locked bedroom door.

The following suggestions will help make it easier for adolescent children to adjust in blended families:

1. Spend time preparing the children for the remarriage. Explore their feelings long before the marriage takes place. Listen to their fears and anxieties. Make provisions for them to be part of the actual remarriage ceremony.

2. Affirm their right to love and expect love from the natural parent with whom they will no longer live. Assure them they are not being disloyal in loving a stepparent and will not lose the love of their natural parent.

3. Allow your adolescent children space in the new family. Give them time to adjust to this new family, even if it takes a couple of years.

4. Recognize that mood swings are normal adolescent behavior and would occur even if both natural parents lived together. Adolescents struggle between dependence and independence as a normal part of their development.

5. Attempt to keep your children in the same school for at least one year after the marriage. This arrangement may create transportation problems, but it makes things easier for the children.

6. Openly discuss the use of the car, insurance, dating behavior, and allowances. Talking about plans for college and amounts of money available helps teenagers plan for their futures.

7. Spend time alone with your natural children as well as with

your stepchildren. Going to a sports event, skiing, or taking a walk together demonstrates your respect and love for them.

8. Continue to celebrate family events such as birthdays, holidays, and school activities. Also worship together in the context of your faith in the home as well as in your church or synagogue.

9. Create an atmosphere where healthy sexual attitudes can prevail. This means showing affection without seductiveness. Set limits on dress, such as wearing a robe when walking about the house. Provide an atmosphere that allows for privacy and freedom in discussing sexuality.

10. Agree on discipline and discuss differences about disciplinary actions in private rather than in front of the children.

11. Encourage contact with the parent living in another home by phone calls, letters, or visits.

12. Build a warm and loving marital relationship. Nurture each other first and then let the love spill over into the lives of your children.

"Now You Have a New Brother and Sister!"

Frederic F. Flach, M.D.

Telling a child that he or she has a *new brother or sister* is one way couples planning to remarry try to break the news to their children. It should come as no surprise that they may run into the same reaction as if they were announcing a baby's birth: *jealousy*.

No matter how promising your new spouse's relationship with your children appears to be, a special insecurity is invariably sparked within all the children. If they are going to live with you, they're bound to wonder and worry how much of their new home is really theirs and how much belongs to the other children who visit, whether they visit often or from time to time. Nor is *home* measured in how many square feet they occupy. Home has to do with attention, birthday celebrations, fair treatment, due respect—even love.

One of the most destructive family situations I have seen consisted of a woman with two small children, a boy and a girl, who married a man with whom she then had two more children, another boy and girl. The extent to which the stepfather favored his own children as they grew was reprehensible. He not only ignored completely the ordinary emotional needs of the two older youngsters, but was often openly and outrageously cruel in the criticisms he heaped on them. For example, at dinner he would repeatedly call his stepson stupid; he often suggested his stepdaughter would end up a "loose woman." Unfortunately, the mother was not strong enough—or perhaps not alert enough—to oppose him. Everyone paid the price. His stepchildren ended up hating him. They were also pressed into a trap of vicious competition with their own half siblings from which they could never emerge.

What if the children are not living with you? What may they imagine and fear? They will be searching for clues that you still love them. They will reach out for attention—sometimes extra attention—to prove the point. They will carefully observe how you treat their stepsiblings who do live with you, what presents they receive, how much you reportedly help them with schoolwork, what trips you take them on. Because they are not part of the regular fabric of your life, they will—until it is proved otherwise—believe the worst. And the worst may be confirmed or contradicted by the remarks they hear from the parent with whom they do live. Competition is a normal thing. So is jealousy. You can't eliminate these emotions, but there's a lot you can do to keep them in line.

First, through word and action you should make clear to the children that you are there for them as always, whether they live with you or apart.

Second, assume they are somewhat insecure with their stepsiblings. Communicating that you are creating a new family structure in which *everyone* belongs sets the stage for exactly that: the formation of a new, coherent, vital equilibrium among all those involved.

Third, give the children a chance to talk with you about how they feel about each other. This is no easy task. You must do so with a reasonable degree of objectivity. Your own children probably will be more verbal on such matters. When you hear about conflicts or clashes between stepsiblings, take a deep breath and try to resist the natural inclination to favor your own. At the same time, keep in mind that there may be a great deal of truth in what they're telling you, and advise them accordingly.

Try to sharpen your empathy—a skill that is at the heart of all good human relationships. Empathy means the ability to put yourself in the other person's place. What would it feel like to be your six-year-old son or your fourteen-year-old stepdaughter? How might you feel you were being treated or should be treated? How might stepsiblings look through a child's eyes? Until science has developed an empathy simulator, you'll have to set time aside to practice empathy on your own and experiment with it in your family. It's well worth the effort.

As time passes, don't be surprised to discover new alliances being formed among stepsiblings. Some may actually seem to exclude natural brothers and sisters. In one instance, I observed a thirteen-year-old girl who was always in relentless competition with her sixteen-year-old sister, whom she mistakenly believed her mother favored. When her mother remarried, she quickly developed a strong friendship with her eighteen-year-old stepsister. They had more in common than did she and her own sister. Once she felt appreciated and understood, her conflicts with her own sister gradually diminished.

When our society was agricultural and transportation difficult, stepbrothers and stepsisters in isolated families often fell in love and married. Although marriages today between stepsiblings are less likely and less necessary, stepsiblings have been known to become the very best of friends. Our responsibility is to establish a family environment in which such friendship can develop.

Teenagers Speak Out about Stepfamily Living
Jeanne Belovitch

The following comments are from a panel of teenagers and one young adult who attended the Fourth Annual Stepfamily Conference in October 1985. Their ages range from thirteen to twenty-one years old. Each has experienced life in a stepfamily. Here's what they have to say:

About Stepparents

When my stepmother came along, I needed her. I don't remember living alone. I didn't think she was going to replace my mother. But I knew I needed her.

You feel they are going to take the place of your real mom. But they don't ever. But you don't ever get over it. I'll never love my stepmother like my real mother.

One of the hardest things for me to do is express gratitude toward my stepmother. I don't know what to do on Mother's Day. I didn't wish either one happy Mother's Day.

I really think I had a bad time with Ellen. She's not a bad person. Even though I didn't know her, I hated her. I didn't get to know her. You need to get to know the stepparent.

She [my stepmother] laid down her hand. She made all these rules. Then I'd take things out on my sister. The rules should have been more gradual.

About Visiting the Biological Parent

We're at my father's house. He wants us to spend all the time with him. But we're out doing yard work. We're pulling weeds somewhere, and he's planting a tree. We're not together.

If I want to see my biological parent, my stepparent will say, "I spent time with you all day." I don't think I'm with my biological parent as much as I'd like when my stepparent is there.

We need more time to be alone with my mom, my dad, and my stepmother. You're not as close when you're in a group.

I think it's important that we get to know each parent . . . that the custodial parent not estrange you from the noncustodial parent.

About the Don'ts and the Dislikes

Don't put us in the middle. . . . They [our parents] *tell us we take sides, then they take sides. I told my parents, I said, "I'm not your messenger anymore."*

To have my parent say my other parent is a jerk doesn't make you feel very good.

Why are we still fighting when we're not living in the same house? I wish you, the parents, could make an extra effort and not embarrass us. If you don't do it for yourselves, do it for us. My graduation day was a little rocky. I was real nervous. My stepmom was real good. We threw this nice party so my mother could meet my friends. My mother only stayed a half an hour. If you could bury these feelings for just a day. Just do it for us.

When you say "I know what you're going through," you really don't. Then my stepparent will give me statistics. It doesn't help. . . .

About the Benefits and Joys

We are learning more about communicating with each other and dealing with other people and a breakup in your home. It makes me stronger for what will happen in later life.

I made the best friend I ever had—my sister. I love my families. Both of them.

I think I've grown. It's neat to start off hating people and grow to love them.

I don't have two parents; I have three parents. We've been through good times and bad times.

It [stepfamily living] *has made us more independent people. We're better people because we've learned how to deal with hurt and pain. And pain makes you care real strong.*

Lessons from the Simple Words of Children

Donna Bilbrey

The following comments are from six children who have experienced divorce in their families and the remarriage of one or both of their parents.

Six-year-old Elaine lives with her mother and visits her father every weekend. Her mother is remarried; her father is not.

> *My daddy picks me up every Friday night after I get home from school. And I like Thursdays best 'cause you know why? 'Cause after Thursday is Friday and on Friday, Daddy comes. I would like to see my daddy every day, but I can't.*

Bill hasn't seen his natural father in seven years. Now fourteen years old, he lives with his mother and stepfather. His stepfather has adopted him.

> *The only thing that really bothers me is the constant court battles that have gone on for eight years between my dad and his ex-wife. They never end, and we're always short on money for fun things because of lawyer bills. I am not ever getting married.*

Jenny, who is ten years old, lives with her maternal grandmother. Her mother died when she was seven. Her father is remarried.

> *I like my stepmom okay, but those kids of hers are wild! I spend two weeks in the summer with them, and I have an okay time. But those kids drive me crazy! It's so noisy there. I come home to Gram's and for a week I don't even turn on my radio. I just feel better with the quiet.*

Tony lives with his mother, who is remarried. He is eight years old. His father is remarried, with two sons. Tony visits his father only at Christmas and during the summer.

> *I miss my dad. But he calls me every week. We live far away from him now, so I don't see him much anymore. I wish my mom and dad would have stayed married.*

Fifteen-year-old Jason lives with his father. He has not heard from his mother in eight years.

Everything is just the way I want it to be. Dad and I have a pretty good time baching it. He has a girl, but she's okay, too.

Kelly, age nine, lives with her mother and stepfather and their three young boys. She visits her father on holidays and during the summer. Her father lives twelve hundred miles away.

I like airplanes. I always fly alone to visit Daddy and it's fun. I would make Mommy and Daddy not hate each other so much because I love them both. I also wish Mom would pack some clothes for me. When I go to Daddy's sometimes it's warm when I leave home. But it's cold when I get to Daddy's. Daddy always takes me straight to the shopping center and buys me what I need.

There are many lessons for parents to learn from the simple words of children. From Jenny, we hear how difficult it is for a child to adjust to different environments during and after a visit. From Kelly, we see how an adult can hurt or embarrass a former spouse through the frailty of a child.

Look and listen to your children, and then do something to change a situation for the better of all involved. Try seeing situations through your children's eyes, and perhaps you will gain in clarity too.

9

Custody, Visitation Rights, and Child Support

The Issue of Custody

Robert S. Weiss

When a father and mother decide to live apart, they also must decide who will remain in charge of the children. Most often they agree it should be the mother.

Our ideas about what is the best custody arrangement, however, have changed radically over the years and are still in flux. Judges in the early nineteenth century—expressing the thinking of their time—held that fathers were the responsible figures in families, with other members subordinate to them. So it followed that when wives left their husbands, which happened infrequently, the husbands should retain custody of the children.

Some years later mothers became the ones fitted by providence for the nurturance of the young, as long as they were not alcoholic, unbalanced, neglectful, or immoral. When parents separated, mothers were the custodial parents of choice.

Today, informed opinion is that neither fathers nor mothers are inherently superior as parents. Almost all states that consider this matter require judges to disregard the gender of the parents when deciding custody.

Nevertheless, in about 90 percent of divorces, it is the mother who receives custody. Because it is usually the mother who has been the parent responsible for child care during the marriage, she is the likely one to continue in that role after divorce. Fathers, believing that their chances in a custody fight remain slim, are reticent to go to court.

About one divorcing couple in ten does bring a custody contest to court. Custody contests produce intense animosity between parents. Even parents who had previously been able to remain relatively friendly become bitter antagonists. They believe they are fighting for the welfare of their children. Whatever the outcome, the fight is likely to leave lasting scars.

Children also suffer when their parents fight in court over their custody. Court-appointed investigators may appear in the children's home at any time to judge the quality of the home. They may interview the children about with which parent they would prefer to live. Until custody is decided, the children's living arrangements remain uncertain, and often their parents are preoccupied with preparing for the next hearing.

One attempt to solve the diffcult problem of custodial decisions is to award the parents *joint custody*. This term has two meanings. One meaning is that both parents retain the rights they always have had as parents—for example, the right to participate in decisions about schooling or summer activities.

In California, *joint custody* based on this first meaning is what a judge will award unless there is reason to act differently. Judges in several states, including Washington, Oregon, and Massachusetts, also may award *joint custody* in this sense.

The other meaning of *joint custody* is that every week, month, or year parents will alternate in providing the children's shelter. This arrangement is also referred to as *joint residential custody*.

Although children whose parents have joint residential custody tend to like it better than other arrangements because it keeps both parents in their lives, it is not suitable for every child. Adolescents often want a single home as a base and find alternating homes confusing. Very young children may absolutely need at least one parent on whom they can always count. Current research suggests that children might be best served if their parents have joint custody in the legal sense, but are not required to alternate residences. At the same time, children should have easy access to the parent with whom they do not live.

Joint custody is one approach to the troublesome problems of custody; whether it is the final word is yet to be decided.

Don't Litigate—Mediate
Marie Kargman

"My husband's ex-wife refused to let his daughter Lisa visit on Sundays like she is supposed to, so he stopped child support. I think this is fair!" Ruth Adams*—present wife of Joe Adams, father of Lisa, age twelve—who thought stopping child support payments was fair, was not prepared for the retaliation by Lisa's mother—a lawsuit. Was *this* fair?

Stopping Lisa's support money put Joe Adams in contempt of court. He had violated the court's order for child support. Nothing in the court's order decreed at the time of the divorce gave Joe the right to stop support if Lisa did not visit as per agreement. Ideally, Lisa's parents should have been in touch with each other if the visiting agreed on was to be interrupted. Lisa or her mother should have told Joe she could not visit on Sundays; alternative arrangements could have been made.

But Lisa's mother and father do not talk to each other. Although Lisa has a good relationship with her father, she does not feel free to call him if her mother objects. Was the courtroom the best forum to resolve this family dispute?

The trial judge assigned to the case of *Adams* v. *Adams* didn't think so. The Adams family had been quarreling in court since their divorce ten years ago. This time, when the lawyers approached the bench, the judge said to them, "I think your clients should try mediation." Both lawyers told the judge their clients couldn't be in the same room together. How could they mediate? "Let them try," said the judge. He recommended that both lawyers arrange for the mediation to take place in my office.

Each lawyer cautioned me: "These are two people who always fight when they talk to each other. They need a referee." Each suggested that I speak to the parents separately. I declined. Parents

---

*All names have been changed in this case.

should be able to learn to talk to each other if they both have the best interests of their child as a goal. The best place for them to begin a talking relationship is in a mediator's office, where each one's rights to talk will be protected. Parents are in a better position to make decisions for and about their children than judges are, and they should have that opportunity. As a family mediator, I try to encourage ex-spouses and their lawyers to dispense with separate meetings and secrets. In a protective climate, each spouse is encouraged to listen with respect. Each gets equal time.

At our first meeting, I learned that what the lawyers had said was true. Edith would not let Joe say more than two or three words. She interrupted, cross-examining him like a district attorney. How did Joe react? After making several tries at finishing a sentence, he simply stopped talking. Having observed the pattern of interaction, I told Edith and Joe that mediation would proceed according to certain rules they would make for themselves. I gave them a little background on what mediation is, what is expected of them, how mediation works, its advantages over court-ordered decisions, and some of the risks of court-imposed ones.

Some of the explanation went like this: Ideally, parents want to make their own decisions about custody, visitation, and support without the intervention of third parties. For some divorced persons, however, this is almost impossible. If an impartial third party is introduced into the talks, parents can and do make their own decisions. Mediation research says that parents who make their own decisions in family matters through mediation are far more successful in arriving at lasting agreements than are parents who live with agreements imposed by courts.

A mediator is not a therapist or a counselor. A mediator is a person trained to help people talk to each other with respect, so they can make their own decisions about resolving their differences or learning to live with them. When two parents agree to mediate, they affirm their confidence in their own maturity. They say, *yes,* we can make decisions for our families. Children feel better, too, when their parents stay out of court—when their parents don't litigate.

People who litigate should know that litigation has more risks than mediation. Lower-court judges' decisions are accountable to an appeals court, and their decisions must relate to the facts presented in the courtroom. Sometimes judges make decisions based on their own sensitivity to the evidence: what the witness expressed—a tone of voice, a certain gesture or look—but did not say. Such nonverbal emotion is not *evidence;* it is not in the record. Appeals courts look for *facts,* and the lower judge's decision may not be upheld, regardless of how wise it is, if the record does not contain facts to support that decision. Sensitivity is not a provable fact!

An appeal represents an additional risk that adds to family disharmony. If the lower-court decision is reversed and remanded for further trial, it means more litigation, more stress, more anxiety, more problems for children to juggle. In mediation, by contrast, there is no risk of appeal. The two parties have only to appeal to themselves. They know what they intended the agreement to be and how they intended it to work. In other words, they know the "legislative history" of their agreement—how it came about—and if it is not working as well as they had hoped, they can try mediation again. Because children's needs change and parents' situations change, a mediation agreement must have flexibility written into it.

With this background information out of the way, each parent agreed not to interrupt the other for ten minutes. During this time, each could make his or her own case. At the end I summarized what I thought they had expressed as their concerns. This list was edited by both parents, and an agenda for discussion was agreed on, always with the caveat that no interruptions would be recognized or responded to. I enforced this agreement between the parties.

Lisa was the subject. The discussion started with visitation. Lisa was now involved in ice skating competitions on Sundays. Sunday, however, was the time Lisa was supposed to visit with her father at his home. Because Lisa's father would not pay for Lisa's ice skating lessons, her mother did not want him to know about the competitions. She didn't want him to see Lisa perform.

Lisa was her father's baby, and he looked forward to her Sunday visits. Her stepmother made plans for each Sunday. Lisa's mother, however, enjoyed her daughter's success as a skater and was not about to share it with her ex-husband. How did Lisa feel?

Both parents agreed to my request to invite Lisa into the mediation process if she wanted to be involved. Our plan was for me to talk with Lisa privately, to explain the mediation process, and to give Lisa the opportunity to attend the mediation conferences.

When Lisa came she was reluctant to talk at first. When I asked, "Do you enjoy your visits with your stepmother?" she answered, "My stepmother is also my aunt. I like her and my cousins." After this disclosure, her talk flowed. Lisa's family lived next door to her mother's brother and his wife and children. Lisa's father divorced her mother; her aunt divorced her uncle. Lisa's aunt became her stepmother. As a mediator, I had new insight into the hostility of Lisa's mother toward her ex-husband and his present wife.

With the consent of Lisa's parents, Lisa now became part of the mediation team. Her opinions were asked and her preferences noted. Both parents were motivated to maintain a good relationship with Lisa.

Two people who could not talk to each other because one of them did not know how to deal with interruptions and domination now learned how to talk about the particular incident that had initially brought them into mediation: withdrawal of visitation and stopping of child support. They also included other visitation problems to reconcile, such as parents' visiting night at school, other school events, and skating performances in which Lisa participated. They talked about the future: graduation, engagement parties, and weddings.

When the mediation concluded, the parents had agreed on a few points: (1) Lisa's summer vacation would include time with each of them, (2) Lisa would go to camp, and (3) in the future, they would notify each other of a change in plans.

All of this was put into writing and signed by both Edith and Joe. A copy of the agreement went to each lawyer. It was then up to the lawyers to dismiss the court action.

The Rights of the Noncustodial Parent

Peter Cyr

The overwhelming number of noncustodial parents are fathers. In fact, according to one of the most commonly cited divorce statistics, over 90 percent of all divorces involving minor children result in sole custody to the mother. This trend seems to be changing, but slowly.

Most divorce decrees state that the noncustodial parent has *reasonable visitation*. What does this term mean? It is interpreted differently by each individual parent, depending on the circumstances. The most common schedule of *reasonable visitation* is every other weekend, plus one nightly visit during the week of the off-week. The result: most noncustodial parents see their children only four days per month, if a weekend is defined as starting on Saturday morning. During the summer months, noncustodial parents can have their children from four to eight weeks. If the children are of school age, additional time is granted during Christmas and spring vacations.

What the question comes down to is: Can noncustodial parents maintain or establish meaningful parenting relationships with their children by exercising reasonable visitation? Common sense indicates that such a task is nearly impossible. It is hard enough to maintain a loving relationship with an adult if you see that person only four days per month. With a young child, it is that much harder.

If there is a dispute concerning the reasonable visitation of the noncustodial parent, what will the court do? Too often the answer is *nothing*. The term *reasonable visitation* is so vague that it is unenforceable. Imagine if divorce decrees simply stated that the noncustodial parent should pay *reasonable* child support. Child support is defined to the penny, which is one reason that it is easier to enforce than visitation is. Even in cases where visitation is clearly defined, however, judges do not enforce it. If they did, mothers would be going to jail.

Another problem for noncustodial fathers is that many end up paying for both sides of any divorce litigation, even when that litigation occurs years after the final divorce decree. Against this background, it is understandable that men are reluctant to pursue visitation rights in court.

If the majority of noncustodial fathers do not take their visitation problems to court, are there state services to help them? Again, the answer is no. In fact, many state agencies refuse even to reveal children's whereabouts to noncustodial parents. Many fathers send their child support checks to post office boxes, and state bureaucracies have no idea where their children are or how they are.

Even when visitation is clearly defined, it still remains relatively easy for custodial parents to deny noncustodial parents access to their children. Many custodial parents move soon after divorce decrees become final. These moves usually make it practically impossible for noncustodial parents to see their children on a regular basis from both a financial and a geographical point of view. Some judges, however, do not tolerate this kind of behavior. If a judge suspects that a custodial parent is moving for punitive reasons, sometimes the judge will rule that the move constitutes a *change of circumstances* and will therefore jeopardize the custodial parent's chances of retaining custody. Such an enlightened judicial attitude does a great deal to discourage frivolous moves.

Other judges have decreed that the custodial parent bear some of the financial responsibility for the move. Financial responsibility can take the form of reduced child support payments, or payment of part or all of the transportation expenses involved in maintaining a meaningful relationship between the noncustodial parent and the children. This latter order does not happen frequently, but it is becoming more common.

The very least that noncustodial parents should expect when their children move is a visitation schedule that accommodates the changes in geographic circumstances.

Often, when noncustodial parents are denied access to their children, they respond by refusing to pay child support. Technically speaking, a noncustodial parent's right to parent the child is not dependent on payment of child support. In visitation denial cases, however, the first determination made by many judges is whether the noncustodial parent is current in child support. If the noncustodial parent has a sharp and aggressive lawyer, the lawyer will object to this line of questioning as irrelevant. Few lawyers voice this objection, however, because they fear they will alienate a judge before whom they must appear on a daily basis.

Is there hope for noncustodial mothers and fathers in the near future? As long as lawyers and judges think in terms of sole custody, the answer is *no*.

Some states are beginning to abandon the concept of custody entirely. Maine statutes speak only in terms of *shared parenting*. Maine law also stipulates that every divorce case involving minor children must be mediated first. If mediation fails, a judge will hear the case, but the judge has the option of sending both parties back to mediation if he or she decides that a *good faith effort* was not made. This nonadversarial approach of compulsory mediation is about two years old in Maine. Also, there seems to be a trend in this state toward joint custody even if one of the parties opposes it.

Joint custody as a way to solve custody disputes appears to hold a great deal of promise for the future. Cases that involve two *fit parents* and no domestic violence can often be resolved by joint custody. Joint custody, however, does not always work. If one parent is determined to be uncooperative, that parent usually succeeds in creating all kinds of havoc. Sometimes in these cases a judge will award sole custody to the most cooperative parent, which helps ensure the children's access to both parents.

It is becoming more and more difficult to ignore the constitutional issues involved in contested custody cases. It has been argued that *fit parents* have a fundamental right to joint custody (see Ellen Canacakos, "Joint Custody as a Fundamental Right," *Arizona Law Review*, Vol. 23, pages 785–800). The Supreme Court of New Jersey, in *Beck* v. *Beck* (NJ 432 A2d 63), says that joint custody may be awarded by a judge even if neither party has requested it, as long as it is in the best interests of the children. Finally, the Maine Supreme Court has ruled in *Cyr* v. *Cyr* (Me 432 A2d 713) that a judge must honor a request for finding-of-facts concerning reasons for deciding custody, if the decree is a final divorce decree and if the request is made in a timely and proper manner.

Using tools such as these, most *fit parents* should be able to preserve their status as *real parents* and not be reduced to Disneyland moms and dads.

On Being a Good Absentee Parent

Peter Cyr

It takes a sustained, conscientious effort to be a good absentee parent. Here are some suggestions that address a variety of situations that an absentee parent may encounter:

1. Make sure the visitation schedule is spelled out. This makes it easier on everyone, including the child. If the divorce decree is nebulous, the visitation rights should be made clear in writing.

2. If your child requires disciplinary action during a weekend visit, don't acquiesce. Try to create stability and reality during weekend visits. Avoid the "Disneyland parent" phenomenon.

3. Don't use your child as a means of finding out what your former spouse is up to.

4. Never criticize the actions of the other parent in front of your child. If you can't think of anything positive to say, the best rule is silence.

5. Always be on time when picking up and dropping off your child. This behavior demonstrates consistency and care.

6. Return the child directly to the other parent or a mutually agreed on third party. Never leave a child alone on a street corner, waiting for the other parent.

7. Keep your communications to a minimum when returning the child to the other parent. This is not the time to discuss problems concerning the child. You can call or write later.

8. Set a time and date for the *next* visit every time you return the child. Be sure the parent as well as the child has this information.

9. Always keep your promises to your child. Don't promise what you can't deliver.

10. Communicate with your former spouse about the child by letter. It's the least threatening form of communication. It also provides a permanent record. The next best way to communicate is by phone.

11. Avoid face-to-face communication about the child between you and your former spouse, unless the conversation can be kept businesslike. Don't attempt small talk; it only leads to game playing.

12. Set aside an area in your home for your child's weekend visits. You can furnish this special space together. Yard sales and secondhand shops offer good buys, and children enjoy these excursions. Ten dollars goes a long way at a yard sale.

13. Finally, a word of warning. When the custodial parent denies visitation, for whatever reason, *don't* terminate your child support payments. It never works. Judges are more likely to listen to a petitioning absentee parent who is current in child support than to one who is not.

Child Support:
A Public *and* Private Problem

Jeanne Belovitch

Since Ronald Reagan signed into law the Child Enforcement Act, states across this country have been cracking down on parents who are behind on child support payments.

The law allows child support agencies to intercept a parent's federal or state tax refund and credit it to his or her delinquent account. In less than a year after the law was passed in 1984, Illinois alone gave to the Internal Revenue Service the names of 42,000 delinquent parents. States also are embellishing the Child Enforcement Act with their own creative collection techniques in going after these large sums of arrearages. For example, percentages of unemployment insurance payments are being intercepted, businesses are cooperating with state agencies in forcing deductions from payrolls, and names of delinquent parents are being given to the media.

As Lynn Wardle, a Brigham Young University (BYU) law professor and adviser of BYU's Family Law Society, said in an interview with the *Salt Lake City Tribune:*

> Child support is no longer a private problem. Since 1965 the divorce rate has doubled, resulting in more single parent families dependent on a third party, a former husband and father, for support. The number of families on public assistance has also increased, making child support a matter of public concern.

This collection fervor may benefit children whose well-being is in jeopardy when payments are withheld. But does all this legislation address the heart of the matter?

Why are so many noncustodial parents (mostly fathers) not making their support payments? Do custody arrangements and visitation rights influence how noncustodial fathers respond to child support? Researchers at several universities in the United States and Canada are looking for answers to these questions.

Recent studies have shown that noncustodial fathers who participate in joint-custody parenting express a real commitment to their children in terms of financial and emotional support. In one study of 200 families, there was less than a 6 percent default on child support payments by joint-custody parents. Also, 85 to 90 percent of these families reported a "highly satisfactory" acceptance of joint custody for themselves and their children. By contrast, in sole-custody families studied, 72 percent of noncustodial fathers defaulted on child support payments.

In another survey of 168 divorced fathers, four out of five non-custodial fathers claimed they would voluntarily increase child support if they were given legal and physical custody and knew their children needed the increase. Four out of five noncustodial fathers also stated that they begrudged paying child support because of their treatment by the legal system.

Are these conclusions shocking? No. It stands to reason that when a noncustodial father in a sole-custody family experiences power struggles with his former spouse masked as visitation disputes, anger and resentment over lack of accessibility in seeing the children, and a biased legal system, a common response is, "I won't give her any more money for the kids!" Unfortunately, children are the victims in this scenario. Sole custody *can be* fertile ground for the expression of anger, resentment, hostility, power struggles, and revenge in the form of delinquent child support.

Although there is no last word on joint custody as the panacea for the custody dilemma, joint custody does provide opportunity for increased communications, accessibility, involvement, commitment, and satisfaction. A noncustodial father and his children who are in a joint-custody arrangement see each other on a regular basis without struggles over visitation rights, and the father's financial and emotional commitment is one of substance. There is no reason for this father to feel compelled to discontinue child support payments, unless he faces an unexpected financial hardship.

Custody, visitation, and child support payments are tied into the same Gordian knot. Legislation is attacking one dimension of the problem. It is up to the individual efforts of custodial and non-custodial parents in their daily lives to cut through this complex problem of delinquent child support in the United States. In turn, increasing numbers of children will receive the care and love they rightfully deserve.

Making Shared Custody Work Well

Patricia L. Papernow

"I like being able to be with both my parents even though they are divorced," says John, whose parents have joint custody of him. "I wouldn't have it any other way," says his father. Recent research tells us that children of divorce do best when they have access to both parents. Denial of contact with one parent can impair a child's development both at the time of divorce and for many years afterward.

Current Massachusetts family law now agrees to awarding shared legal custody in all cases except where there is misconduct. Even when one parent is awarded legal custody, both parents have legal access to medical and academic records as well as the right to *reasonable visitation*.

"No longer is the mother automatically more equal under the law than the father," says attorney Alice Alexander of the Divorce Consultation Service in Brookline, Massachusetts. Even life-style variations such as homosexuality and unmarried cohabitation cannot automatically eliminate a parent from gaining custody. A contesting spouse must prove a parent is clearly unfit.

Whether a divorced couple has shared legal custody of their children, where both parents have equal input on major decisions, or one parent has legal custody with the other parent having only visitation rights, specific physical custody arrangements can be designed to fit each family's needs. Some children spend half the week at each parent's home. Others alternate weeks. Still others find alternating school semesters the best way for them.

Emmie spent her elementary school years living at her father's home during the week and spending weekends with her mother, who was a graduate student in another state. As a teenager, Emmie now lives with her mother, who has returned to Emmie's hometown. David, whose parents have both remarried, spent alternate weeks with each parent for eight years until a drop in his high school grades prompted an all-family conference. After much discussion, David decided to live with his father for the remainder of high school. He said: "It's hard enough being a teenager with two parents to deal with. Four is just too many."

Devising visitation arrangements that suit the changing needs of children and adults is one part of making shared custody work well. Perhaps the greatest challenge for parents who share custody of their children, however, is separating the role of parent from that of spouse. Dr. Harry Keshet of the Riverside Family Counseling Center in Newton, Massachusetts, said: "You have to be able to remember that one can be a terrible spouse and a great parent. I think the key ingredient is being able to accept that whatever happened in the divorce is past."

The following guidelines are suggested for making shared custody work well for all members of the family, particularly children:

1. *Keep conversations between you and your former spouse focused on the children.* Unresolved issues from the marriage, intimate details of daily living, even ups and downs on the job should be shared with friends or new partners. Dr. Keshet says: "Keep it practical rather than personal. Don't talk about your relationship or your love life. Do talk about changing schedules, money issues, and the kids' education." If the relationship with your former spouse is full of conflict, other strategies for minimizing personal involvement are: keep face-to-face contact to a miminum, create a specific time for telephone conversations about children, and confine pickups and dropoffs to brief encounters at the doorway.

2. *Do not share negative feelings about your former spouse with the children.* Listening to parents demean each other is profoundly disturbing to children of any age. The desire to dump on a former spouse becomes especially attractive when a child complains about the *other* parent. But siding with children against a former spouse undermines their self-esteem and entangles them in an impossible loyalty conflict. Ultimately this conflict will damage your own relationship with your children.

When a child complains about a parent, try to make statements empathizing with both the child and your former spouse. With this approach, your child will not be pulled into your personal conflicts. For example: "I'm sorry your mom yelled at you for being late. That must have made you feel awful. She must have been really panicked." Then go complain about your former spouse to your new partner, lover, or friend—out of the children's earshot.

3. *Keep your children's two households separate but equal.* The trick is to acknowledge the differences between your children's two households without demeaning their other parent, even when you disagree strongly with your former spouse. For example: "In your mom's house, you can watch as much TV as you want to, but you can't swear. In our house, you are limited to two hours of television, but you can swear as long as you aren't mean to other people." When children say, "But Mom lets me . . .," you can say, "I know. We disagree about that."

Shared custody works best when former spouses do not interfere with each other's daily decision making about the children. If Dad says no allowance for a week, then Mom shouldn't send money! When there are major issues, such as drug use or failing grades, all adults in the family may need to agree on rules or come to a decision that will support the child's best interest.

4. *Resist the temptation to communicate with your former spouse through your children.* Asking children to convey important information, particularly about parental disagreements ("Tell your dad I don't like his curfew," or "Tell your mom she's spending my money on stupid things") places an unfair and hurtful burden on your children. If it is a major issue, communicate directly with your former spouse. If it's minor, grumble to your new partner or a friend.

5. *Use other adult go-betweens if necessary.* If former spouses cannot engage in co-parenting issues without recreating old emotional conflicts, a stepparent may be able to take on the role of negotiator on difficult issues. Other ways to handle unresolvable conflicts include mediation or sessions with a good family therapist with some knowledge of stepfamily systems.

6. *Pay special attention to the beginnings and ends of visits.* The beginnings and the ends of visits are stressful for all concerned. As one stepmother said: "When the children arrive, I definitely become

the outsider. We have found it makes all the difference if my husband and I have an intimate *date* just before his kids visit."

Many families find that beginnings of visits go more easily when the children and their biological parent have time alone together when they first arrive. Many children also need special time at the end of visits, when they are preparing to disengage from one household and engage with another. Some children need extra withdrawal time; others need time alone with their biological parent; still others simply need space to be anxious and upset. The challenge is to keep experimenting until you find what works for all the people in your family, including stepparents.

7. *Do not create competition between the stepparent and the other parent of the same sex.* The urge to have your new partner replace your former spouse in your child's heart is strong, as is the fear that your former spouse's new partner will replace you. Although these wishes and fears are normal, acting on them creates an impossible dilemma for your child. "If I love my mother, can I love my dad's new wife?" is how it goes for many children in remarried families. Children need permission and reassurance from *all* concerned that they can maintain their special relationships with each of their parents and still have room to develop new kinds of relationships with their stepparents.

Many of these guidelines require a tremendous amount of self-discipline. As one of my clients said, "Doing what comes naturally almost always makes a mess for me in this stepfamily business!" Nevertheless, for adults who can bear the anxiety of sharing children with another and different family, joint custody provides a kind of extended family that is rare in American life today.

Jane, a divorced mother, puts it this way: "Who else could we send the kids to when we go on vacation, knowing they will be cared for, if not exactly in the same way I would, certainly with the same degree of concern and love I have for them." For remarried couples, visitation agreements offer precious time alone without children. Barry, a father with joint custody of his own children, says of his wife, whose children never visit their father: "Sure wish her ex-husband was more involved. I never have a moment alone with her!"

Furthermore, children whose parents can support their relationships with two households without dividing their loyalties have an opportunity to experience two sets of values, relationships, aesthetics, and rhythms of daily living. Also, when parents recouple, children gain access to a much wider variety of adult relationships and role models. Although joint custody creates unique challenges, it offers many benefits to all members of the remarried family.

The Experiences of Parents Who Share Custody

Kathleen Walker

The key to a successful joint custody arrangement is respect for your spouse, says Joan.

You also need money, says her former husband, Geoff.

Two other important factors, they both say, are a commitment to putting your children's interests first and similar attitudes about raising kids.

Joan and Geoff have been separated for two years. Like the other couples in this article, they don't want their real names used.

Unlike many separated couples, where custody of the children is usually with the mother, Joan and Geoff have a fifty–fifty joint-custody arrangement.

Their two children, aged seven and nine, switch houses every Monday, as do the housekeeper and the cleaning woman. Fortunately, Joan and Geoff live within blocks of each other, so the children attend the same school and have the same friends they had before the separation.

Expenses such as education costs, clothing, sports uniforms, and summer camp fees are shared on a prorated basis, based on each parent's salary. Holidays and business trips are negotiated.

All that takes money. Keeping two households is expensive, says Geoff. It's not just a matter of two sets of clothes for the children, it also means more toys and two houses in the same desirable neighborhood.

"I think you can only opt for joint custody if you don't have a money problem," he says. "You have to be in an economic stratum that allows the kids to have a similar setup in both houses—and that's expensive."

Joint custody also requires that both parents be mature in their dealings with each other.

Originally, says Geoff, Joan wanted sole custody. "But I said no way. I was just as involved with parenting as she was." The two then opted for joint custody.

"I read every research paper and book available at the time on joint custody and co-parenting," says Joan. "Geoff and I worked out an agreement before we even went to a lawyer.

"It was, I suppose, the rational side of our lives; meanwhile the crying and the tears about our own relationship was going on. You just have to put your kids above your personal problems."

Putting the kids first also meant figuring out how to break the news that Mommy and Daddy weren't going to live together anymore. For Geoff and Joan, that meant a trip to a child psychologist for help in explaining the situation to their children and to reassure them that they weren't at fault.

"We were obviously very concerned parents before our marriage broke up," says Joan. "Geoff and I talk every day on the phone when the parent who doesn't have the kids that week calls them in the morning."

The first year after the separation was rugged, she admits. "I used to cry Sunday nights when I packed their bags."

On the flip side, she adds, joint custody does give each parent time to him- or herself. "Geoff has a whole week to do his own thing and he loves it," says Joan.

"That's when I get my work done," adds Geoff. "But the kids know the house is always open to them, so they occasionally pop over."

It took a while for the children to adjust to the new schedule of one week at Daddy's and one week at Mommy's. "It's still hard for their friends to remember just where they are on a given week," adds Joan.

But the children's friends weren't the only people affected by Joan and Geoff's separation. Besides the couple's friends, their parents took a while to adjust to the new life-style.

"That first year was a period of adjustment for everyone—especially for friends and in-laws," says Joan. "Geoff and I have tried as much as possible to maintain good relationships with the children's grandparents. It's important for both the kids and the grandparents."

Gradually, she adds, everyone has come to terms with the separation. Occasionally, she says, her youngest child will express his concern at not having both parents under one roof. And she and Geoff find they have to answer a lot of "why" questions. "Like 'Why don't you and Daddy live together?' and 'Why do I have to go to Mommy's house today?' You have to be very sensitive to their needs and thoughts, but you also have to be disciplined so you don't fall for the old 'Well, Daddy lets us do that' ploy," says Joan.

That's why, she adds, sharing the same parenting values is important. "Otherwise it can become adversarial.

"Geoff and I are divided in terms of houses, but we're not divided in terms of spirit. He is, in fact, one of my best friends."

Joint custody for Dawn and Mike is a matter of making the best of a bad situation. It means the two parents must have occasional conversations even though they prefer not to talk to each other.

Despite their personal animosity, the two fought hard for joint custody of their son Peter, now four. "Our marriage broke up when Peter was two," says Dawn. "And it was because he was so young and because Mike was an involved father that we went for joint custody. A child that young tends to forget who people are, and I was afraid that under a sole custody arrangement, Peter would be terrified when Mike picked him up every second weekend."

The most difficult aspect of joint custody, she adds, is the lack of support for the arrangement by family and friends. "My family and friends felt I should have sole custody, and Mike's family and friends thought he should get it because of Peter's sex. My mother, even now, doesn't think we're doing the right thing. Their lack of understanding made things difficult. You'd find yourself defending the other person even when you didn't particularly want to."

Joint custody, she adds, is also hard "because you're not closing the door on the past. You have to deal with each other more than you might otherwise have to. We aren't friends, but I think if either one of us needed help the other would be there."

Mike and Dawn's situation is complicated by distance. Unlike

Geoff and Joan, Mike and Dawn live in different parts of the Ottawa area. It makes getting Peter to and from each other's homes, and to swimming and gymnastics classes, more awkward. "For the past two years Mike and I have been running around like fools making sure Peter gets to everything—always with the knowledge that if we let up for a minute the other one would go for sole custody at the drop of a hat."

Peter lives one week with his mother and one week with his father. He has a set of clothing at both houses, double the toys, two bikes, and two sets of friends.

Both parents have since become involved with other partners. Dawn has remarried and has two children. Mike plans to remarry this fall. "Neither of us reacted very well when another person entered the picture. But at least the four of us share the same background. We know that Peter will have the same kind of home environment in both houses."

Next fall Peter starts school halfway between his parents' houses in a school district in which neither parent lives. At that time his schedule will change to two weeks with his father and two weeks with his mother.

So far, says Dawn, joint custody has been a positive experience for Peter. "He really has the best of everything—more friends, more toys and four 'parents' who are educated and involved with him. He's always very excited to go to either house. There can't be any back-stabbing in a joint custody set up. In fact, Mike and I have worked harder to be nice to each other since we split than we ever did during our marriage."

Laura is forty-five and has been married twenty-three years. She's Catholic and has five children, aged thirteen to twenty. Two and a half years ago she left her husband. "I didn't feel I was getting enough from the relationship—that the communication level just wasn't there," she says.

Her decision took the family by surprise. Her two oldest children still have problems with the fact their mother is no longer home. The three youngest children, although they don't particularly like the situation, have come to terms with it.

Once a week, on Sunday nights, they move back and forth between their father's house and their mother's new townhouse. They bring their clothes, books, and the family cat.

Birthdays are celebrated at both houses. Christmas Eve is spent at one house, Christmas Day at the other. They alternate March breaks with one parent or the other.

Laura and her husband aren't legally separated, nor do they have a legal joint-custody agreement. Like hundreds of other couples, they have come to an unofficial agreement to share the children and share financial burdens such as the mortgage on the family home. Laura believes it costs each parent about $1,200 a month to live separately.

The two youngest children, Sarah and Rachel, say the week-on, week-off set up is the easiest arrangement possible. "We get to see both parents, and switching houses offers a change of scenery," says Sarah, adding that their situation isn't all that unusual. "Only two of my friends have parents who are still together. But we're the only ones involved in joint custody. No one understands the benefits of being able to be with both parents. All they see is the pain of having to carry all your stuff from one house to the other."

On the plus side, Laura says the week she has with her children permits her to enjoy them more. "We communicate better and more easily now," she says. "On the week they're with their father, I get of lot of work done and take time to see friends and go out for dinner." She also has "a relationship—but only when the kids aren't with me."

She believes it's very important for children to have equal time with both parents unless one or the other is abusive. The girls agree. Rachel says that if her marriage ever broke up, she would push for joint custody. But neither has any thoughts about eventually having a family.

"I feel more negative about marriage now," says Sarah. "Not too many people stay together these days."

10

Closing the Gap between the Schools and Stepfamilies

Remarriage and Schools: Support or Sabotage

Elizabeth Einstein

Eight-year-old Erica and her classmates are making plaster-of-paris handprints as a Mother's Day present. As she paints the final coat, Erica is concerned about something. She walks shyly up to her teacher, pulls her aside, and asks for materials to make another one. Mrs. Brown doesn't ask why but simply tells her, "No, each child makes one." Erica looks sad and walks away. Her concern? Should she give the gift to her mother or to her stepmother?

Sensitive educators who are aware of the stepfamily's special dynamics can respond to your family with support. Too often, however, in the school–home partnership, an information gap exists concerning the family. A teacher who lacks awareness about a student's home life may sabotage a sensitive situation, as Mrs. Brown did because she was unaware of Erica's concern about who should receive her gift. Communication between the school and your stepfamily is crucial. When it is nonexistent or unclear, your child's development can be hindered and loyalty conflicts like Erica's intensified.

Educators must address the reality of remarriage and how it affects their students. Today, nearly one-third of the children in American classrooms are involved in some sort of step-relationship. That figure will continue to grow: it is estimated that of all the children born during the 1970s, almost half will experience divorce. Most of these will become stepchildren. Teachers are among the first to deal with children as they cope with troublesome transitions. Since children spend most of their day in school, the classroom can be a stabilizing force for them.

Divorce ends a marriage, but it does not end a family. It does, however, alter its form, and sometimes schools get caught in the process as families make transitions. As common as remarriage is today, a school–stepfamily gap still exists, showing up in the classroom or in educational policies. When textbooks portray only the never-divorced family, children living in nontraditional families feel left out. A *one-home* view intensifies loyalty conflicts when teachers limit the number of gifts made for parents or tickets to the school play or graduation. Children feel forced to choose.

School authorization forms are designed for one home with two biological parents. When no signature line appears for stepparents, it sets up two choices: biological parents can deal with the school and exclude the stepparent, or stepparents can sign the form but must be deceitful about their roles. Report cards and school notices are rarely sent to two homes.

School conferences can also spell disaster. If a teacher feels uncomfortable with divorced or remarried parents, the meeting focuses on coping with these intrusive feelings rather than the child's academic progress. School counselors and nurses who understand the family configurations in which their students live may be better able to help that child.

Teachers need to be sensitive to what they say in the classroom, administrators to the policies they set. Since language reflects and determines beliefs, the words a teacher uses to describe nontraditional families will affect their students. Expressions to be avoided are *broken home, shattered families, natural parent*, and *marriage failure*. Words like *stepmother* and *stepfather* can be integrated into classroom conversations to normalize life for children living in stepfamilies. Principals and school board members need to be aware of how they interpret the Buckley Amendment (1975 Family Educational Rights and Privacy Act) so they are not excluding a noncustodial parent's involvement with the school.

Closing the chasm between the schools and the stepfamily begins with the parents. Although it is the responsibility of the school to respond to the stepfamily and to support it, educators need parents to cooperate by telling them what is happening at home that may affect their youngsters' ability to learn. Schools can make it easier for parents to respond by sending them a memo about obtaining this information. Here are some suggestions that may help make the stepfamily–school liaison a cooperative one:

Reveal any changed status in your family by letter or phone.

Clarify relationships and responsibilities. Who has the right to interact with your child? To take the child from school?

Decide who receives school communications and report cards—one home or two homes.

Determine how many parents and stepparents will attend school conferences and other functions.

Get suggestions from your children on how they think the school can serve them better. If your children get support from a counselor or hear a teacher use negative language about stepfamilies, have them tell you about it.

Noncustodial Parents: You Have Legal Rights with the Schools

Jeanne Belovitch

Most parents are interested in their children's school work. But noncustodial parents, typically fathers, often find getting information about their children's progress in school quite difficult. Many school systems consider them outsiders with few rights—or none.

Noncustodial parents do have certain legal rights. Unless there is a court order or other legal documents to the contrary, the 1974 Family Educational Rights and Privacy Act (FERPA) requires that school districts provide the custodial parent *and* the noncustodial parent with access to records. Your state may offer broader provisions to this law.

FERPA says:

You can obtain information from your child's records on a regular basis if you submit periodic requests. The school must respond within forty-five days.

You can request that the school send you copies of your child's records if a visit to the school is impractical because of distance.

You have the right to see school records if they are kept and the right to a reasonable request for an explanation and interpretation of the record.

You do not need permission from the custodial parent to obtain school records. You have full access to them.

FERPA also requires a school district to:

Provide a parent with the opportunity to correct records believed to be inaccurate.

Obtain from the parent written permission before disclosing information contained in educational records.

11

Holiday Celebrations Begin New Traditions

Wishing for a Kodak Christmas

Robert S. Weiss

A couple of years ago after the Christmas school break, I met in the office of a high school guidance counselor with a dozen or so students, each of them a child of parents who had divorced. We talked about their Christmases.

"I'll tell you," one girl said, "I came down in the morning and our front room looked so pretty with the tree and the tinsel and the lights and gifts. And my mother was there and my brother was there. And I felt so bad because my father wasn't there. I mean, I'm used to him not being there; but we've got this scene, like this Kodak family, except he's not in the picture."

Christmas celebrates families. Its central religious image is a family image—at first a homeless, wandering family, to be sure, but then with a child whose presence, even in a manger, is a focus for familial warmth. The secular images of Christmas are even more strikingly familial: gift-giving among family members, sitting down with the whole family to Christmas dinner. Christmas, like Thanksgiving, is a day when family members come together.

No wonder that in single-parent homes, Christmas is a time of mixed feelings. There can be warmth, but for many there is an awareness of loss and of feeling different from others. Nor does it help to see constantly happy, smiling, two-parent families on television and in newspaper advertisements.

Remarriage makes celebrating Christmases better, but these families have problems to resolve, too. Separated and divorced parents must decide whose household will have Christmas and at what time. To achieve fairness, planning sometimes can get intricate: this year, Christmas Eve and the following morning at father's house; the rest of the day at mother's; next year, the other way; gifts at both homes.

Children who have had back-to-back celebrations, going from Christmas dinner at one parent's home to Christmas supper at the other's, say it is difficult to manufacture the same enthusiasm the second time around. Parents on the latter end of the celebration should be aware of this dilemma for their children.

Christmas also is a time when children are likely to visit the non-custodial parent. For the visiting children it can be distressing to see their biological parent enmeshed in a foreign home. If there are step-brothers and stepsisters who live in the home all the time, the visiting children may have the painful feeling of having been displaced by these other children.

Stepparents have complaints, too. The visiting children may act up a bit. They are likely to feel uncomfortable in the new setting, and they may need reassurance that their biological parent still cares. For the same reasons, they may try to get the biological parent off to themselves, sometimes to the stepparent's annoyance. And because the children's biological parent wants the children to enjoy their brief visit as much as possible, he or she is apt to be especially loving and attentive to them. The stepparent can easily feel annoyed by the children's demandingness and by their partner's indulgence.

Remarried parents tend not to talk about these tensions. Instead, as the holiday season goes on, they become more and more irritable with each other, more and more distant from each other.

Remarried parents who have overcome these difficulties say that resolving them requires mutual understanding and acceptance. This kind of harmony evolves from each telling the other his or her needs and concerns. It can be painful to face problems openly, but otherwise they won't be dealt with.

Christmas in the remarried family can be as warm and rewarding as the Christmases pictured in the Kodak commercials. Indeed, it can be even more rewarding, for there will be much more awareness of how precious—and how deserving of effort—is a caring family.

The Challenge of Holiday Celebrations

Elizabeth Einstein

Soon after they put the tree in the living room, they knew they were in trouble. Anchored in its stand, the long-needled spruce remained bare. Days later, family members were still arguing about how it should be decorated and whether they should open presents on Christmas Eve or Christmas morning.

This was the first Christmas this new stepfamily was to spend together. He was widowed with four children; she was divorced with two youngsters. Married less than a year, each family had a very different notion about how to celebrate Christmas, especially about how to decorate the tree. I asked them to let me know what they finally decided to do.

A week later they did. Since they could not agree on how to dress the tree, they divided it down the middle. One group stood on one side of the tree decorating with popcorn strings, cranberry loops, and paper ornaments. The others trimmed their side with golden balls, tinsel, and lights. They agreed it was strange-looking, but neither family would budge from their traditions. The next year, after they had begun to feel like a family, they made compromises: some new ornaments, and a commitment to make the season more joyous. Rather than a his-and-hers concoction, this stepfamily finally created their first *ours* tree.

Although not all remarrieds have such trouble decorating their first tree, most share a similar story about their first holiday season together. Whether the scenarios reflect differences about food, present choices, or visitation schedules, many agree that what was to be a first time of love, joy, and great expectations became more terrible than terrific. Remarrieds explain that future holidays got better, but it took more than crossed fingers and high hopes. Good planning, lots of communicating, and compromising were required. "If only we'd known in the beginning," most lament or laugh.

Holidays should be joyful times. But as people in any kind of family come together to celebrate, stress from travel or difficult relationships often tarnishes their expectations or dreams. *Planning* is the key to getting your holiday off on the right foot. The remarried family's widened sphere of relationships creates chances for more strain because children may be expected to spend the holiday with Mom's family *as well as* Dad's. Everyone wants a piece of the children and, as the deals are struck and the dates set, the holidays become both exhilarating and exhausting—especially for the youngsters.

Moving between families means that children can practice traditions from the old family at the same time they make new ones in the new family. But melding two ways requires careful negotiating and patience. Will stockings be hung on Christmas Eve and presents opened Christmas morning? Where will the children have dinner: at Mom's or Dad's, or shuttled to both? In multireligious stepfamilies, is Christmas or Hanukkah celebrated, or both?

Becoming a stepfamily takes time—a lot more time than most people realize. Research shows that stepfamilies pass through a series of stages which are normal, before they stabilize and develop a sense of *we*. This is especially important to realize in reducing stress during the holidays. When new stepfamilies try to cope with both the difficulties of becoming a family and the normal stresses associated with holiday time, pressures are bound to be high.

Roots, memories, and traditions are important to all families. During the holidays, then, remarried families have two strikes against them: their roots are fragile and their memories few. They share no common history; indeed, their traditions may be quite diverse. Working out these differences requires advance planning. Waiting to take out two boxes of tree ornaments—"ours" and "theirs"—until it's time to trim the tree courts trouble. Talking long before Christmas about how things were done in former families is wise and starts family members thinking about creative compromises. Sharing traditions and discussing which ones still hold warm memories gets family members talking and exploring why they do certain things. Sometimes we repeat traditions over and over simply *because*, although they have long since lost their real significance.

As new stepfamilies forge their futures, they can create new traditions. Often, during the breakdown of former families, few joint activities continued and holidays without love became especially stressful. Building new traditions provides good opportunities for the new stepfamily to gain a hold on intimacy.

Remarrieds must acknowledge that certain things about their holidays are going to be different. Focusing on the good that remains and the stepfamily's strengths is most productive. Looking at what's special can make a difference in lifting spirits during an otherwise difficult time, when feelings of sadness surface.

Research shows that although children of divorce do deal with many challenges, they are not unhappy about all the extra holiday dinners, presents, and attention they get. According to Dr. Frank Furstenburg of the University of Pennsylvania, who studies the effect of the extended family on the stepfamily, the key is how well adults can handle this situation. How well people have resolved their differences with former spouses and stopped using children to settle these differences is a good mirror on what's happening in their stepfamily living.

Holidays can be an enriching time for children of remarriage. As youngsters move between two families, their horizons are broadened. As they travel to new places, stepchildren can meet new people and learn new experiences. They become more flexible and adaptable. They have more role models from whom they can learn attitudes, beliefs, and skills. And, of course, sharing diversities can be enriching. Much depends, again, on attitude, which begins with the adults setting the tone.

When youngsters travel great distances to be with their other parent, the success of the holiday visit rests with their parents. At one end, the children need to be prepared. Acknowledge their feelings and let them know you feel good about their leaving to be with their other parent. The receiving parent needs to help the children feel comfortable with the transition during this sensitive time, when they might want to be with their familiar surroundings and friends. One way to integrate children who do not live in your house year round is to get them involved. Don't treat them like guests. Give them some tasks and responsibilities so they soon feel part of that family, too.

Christmas is a time of expectations for all of us. Unmet ones account for much of the sadness and postholiday depression. An emphasis on creating realistic holiday expectations will prepare remarried families to receive the gifts the holiday can offer. When hopes and dreams are tempered with reality, a joyful exchange of sharing old traditions while making new ones can provide a festive foundation for the future. The holiday message offers hope and love. With these blessings, most things are possible for the remarried family.

How to Work toward
Realistic Holiday Expectations

1. *Plan ahead.* Start right now to plan *when* activities will take place, *where* they will take place, and *who* will participate. To avoid schedule conflicts, grandparents should be consulted. Early gift suggestions may avoid competitive gift giving or duplicates.

2. *Lower expectations, honor realities.* For those in new remarried families, a certain sadness over what no longer can be often emerges. Awareness that this sadness is normal helps you get through it. Since little else is the same about your family, expecting the holidays to be as they once were is courting disappointment. See the differences as strengths and as enriching.

3. *Respect loyalties.* Until stepgrandparents develop a relationship with the new children in their lives, they may be uncomfortable deciding what role to play with them. Part of that unease may result in unequal gift giving and special treatment of biological grandchildren. Talk to the children, helping them not to personalize this need. It takes time for relationships to grow.

4. *Be creative.* Rather than expecting to repeat everything as it once was, have each family member explore which traditions really continue to have special meanings, and continue only those. Brainstorm together new ones that will represent *our* way. This is a way of savoring the best from each family's past, enriching each other's present, and building new traditions for the stepfamily's future.

12

When There Are Racial or Religious Differences

The Challenges of Making It as an Interracial Stepfamily

David A. Baptiste, Jr.

Although there continues to be opposition to marriages across racial lines, an improving racial climate in the United States has led many men and women to remarry outside of their racial/cultural groups.

These remarriages—highly complex in nature—present special challenges for the entire family. If you are an interracial/intercultural stepfamily or are planning to become one, here are some of the difficulties of which you should be aware. It is important to remember, however, that not all intermarried stepfamilies experience these issues.

1. *Disapproval.* Often intermarried stepfamilies experience disapproval of their marriages. Extended family members, especially parents, may object to their child's marriage for racial or cultural reasons. Other members fear this kind of marriage is damaging to their children because of how society views these relationships. Another concern is that the stepfather, who is of another race or culture, will adopt the children. For whatever reasons extended family members disapprove, their attitudes, feelings, and behavior

can compound the usual stress and conflicts in this family. If the remarried couple do not deal effectively with the disapproval of extended family members, the marriage can be placed in jeopardy.

2. *Adjusting to spouse and children.* A husband or wife may find adjusting to step living with a racially or culturally different spouse and children difficult. These couples should be alert to convenient masking of family problems with the excuse of *cultural differences.* Because of the double stress of remarriage and intermarriage, it is important that couples sort out their marital differences in terms of what is cultural and what is personal. For example, money management is a personal, not a cultural, difference.

3. *Overcoming previously learned prejudices.* Many spouses may be unaware of their attitude toward the racial or cultural group of their new spouse until challenged. Regardless of a spouse's respect for these cultural differences, each partner brings to the marriage a residue of learned stereotypes and beliefs about other racial and cultural groups.

When these stereotypes and beliefs continue, they can influence attitudes and behavior in the marriage through subtle manifestations such as facial expressions, gestures, or unspoken expectations about how a spouse should or shouldn't behave. This kind of situation provides more than the usual potential for conflict.

4. *Children from mixed racial/cultural backgrounds.* Another conflict for stepfamilies arises when the spouses are of the same background, but there are children of a mixed racial or cultural background from a previous marriage. Often the stepparent is unable or unwilling to overcome learned prejudices toward the particular group of which the stepchild is, in part, a member.

5. *Disapproval from the noncustodial father.* Children in interracial stepfamilies deal with their share of adversity. To begin, it is not easy for them to grow up in a family that at its best may be marginally accepted in the community. They also must contend with disapproval from the noncustodial father. Some noncustodial fathers object to their children being parented by a male of another race or culture. Others fear living in an intermarried family is unhealthful for their children and creates too many difficulties for them.

Although there are special challenges to living in an intermarried stepfamily, these families can succeed. To do so, however, it is important that spouses increase their own communications, learn to maintain distinct boundaries between their immediate family and their respective extended families, and learn to maintain open communication with their respective children from previous relationships. For example, although it is not necessary for parents to obtain their children's approval to remarry, they should inform their children of their decision to intermarry before the marriage takes place. This provides an opportunity for parents to deal with the children's initial concerns and to minimize later objections.

Finally, it is important that spouses accept each other's cultural differences. They should make allowances for the behaviors of the other's culture, rather than interpreting them as inappropriate, which may increase marital and family conflict.

The Remarried Family with Two Faiths

Bernard Bloomstone

Unless a married couple of different faiths divest their life of all religious observances, they are certain to experience conflict at one point or another. The view that mature individuals can resolve all problems amicably through reason and logic fails to take into account the emotional factors bound up with religious observances.

No Christian can relate to the family gathering at Christmas dinner in a dispassionate and rational way. No Jew can help but feel emotional when considering the family sitting around the Passover Seder table. To confront the emotion is the challenge.

Consider the following hypothetical situation. Let's assume two individuals remarry who are nominally committed to different faiths. Assume also that each spouse has young children who were introduced to and taught the fundamentals of their respective faiths before the remarriage occurred. If you asked these children, "What faith are you?" they would reply, "I'm Jewish" or "I'm Christian." Finally, let's assume the couple agreed that, when they married, each individual within the household would maintain his or her own particular religious identity.

The above situation prompts several difficult questions. I'll present two of them here:

Can such a family live under one roof without experiencing religious conflict? If nonreligious conflict among individuals is inevitable, we can conclude that deeply rooted religious teachings and practices will result in emotionally charged arguments.

Who is to settle a religiously oriented dispute? The stepparent? Would the child regard the stepparent's solution to the problem biased?

Remarried families with two faiths face a volatile situation that can threaten the serenity of a home and the kind of relationship a remarried couple want for themselves.

I recall one first marriage where the wife converted to Judaism. As long as there were no children, the Jewish husband did not mind visiting his non-Jewish in-laws to exchange gifts on Christmas Day. But when children were born and when the little ones reached the age of understanding, this man grew angry as Christmas and Christmas dinner with the in-laws approached. The wife had to walk on eggshells during the holiday season, which was no way to foster a healthy relationship between these two adults.

A similar reaction can occur in any remarriage with two faiths, especially when children are involved. If religious identity plays even a minimal role in the parents' life, it is likely that the parents will become hostile when they feel their offspring's identities face a challenge or a threat.

Are there solutions? Is a home with children where two faiths prevail doomed to conflict? Obviously, there are no pat answers. Each person in a remarried family of two faiths is an individual with a particular background, which influences and determines levels of patience and tolerance.

Most important, however, is that couples be cognizant of the pitfalls they face. Couples must realize that reactions to religious issues are seldom based on theological or philosophical differences, but are usually emotional reactions. When dealing with younger children, couples must also realize that children see things only in black and white, not in shades of gray. As a result, they are not as flexible as one might wish when it comes to religion. Thus the best advice for remarried couples of two faiths is: *exercise extreme caution.*

A household whose children have reached a degree of emotional maturity may be less likely to face some of the challenges confronting the multireligious home with younger children. Grown children, however, stir up different fears for their parents. Whom will my child date? Whom will my child marry? What will the religion of my child's in-laws be?

In the many interfaith married couples I know, I often hear parents express a desire that their children marry within their own faith. Should we assume partners in a mixed marriage feel guilty for having married outside *their* faith? Do they yearn for vicarious atonement through their child? These fears, however, are quite personal and generally do not spill over to taint day-to-day living.

All in all, multireligious marriages, whether they be first or second ones, can present a mixed bag of serious complications. It takes great skill to resolve some of these problems to the couple's mutual satisfaction.

13

From the
Roman Catholic Church

Current Positions
on Divorce and Remarriage

James J. Young

1. The Roman Catholic understanding of marriage is grounded in the age-old understanding that human married love, by its very nature, hungers for permanent commitment. The ancient Jews came to this understanding, as is evident in the Hebrew Scriptures, and Jesus took this understanding as his own. So the Catholic Church teaches that if a couple wish to enter into a true Christian union, they must intend and be able to commit themselves to each other for life. For this reason the Church strives diligently to help couples marry well and to prevent divorce.

2. The Church sees Christian marriage as a human commitment between two partners, which is a true marriage when it is characterized by the normal aspects of any human marriage—love, affection, mutual respect, fidelity, perseverance. It is the religious faith of the two partners that makes a human marriage a Christian marriage. Religious faith enables the couple to see an even greater significance in their relationship: their love for one another is a sign in human history of God's own love for humankind. It is the experience of human, married love that enables Christians to glimpse the nature of God's faithful love.

3. Even though the Church offers a variety of marriage preparation programs to help couples marry well, recent experience has taught that many couples marry unwisely, choosing partners who lack the requisite human resources to build a lasting marriage commitment. If a marriage celebrated in the Church breaks down because of such human deficiencies, the Church frees couples from the obligations of that marriage by the process of *annulment.* An annulment is a decision by the Church that even though two people sincerely began a lifelong marriage commitment, there was something lacking in one or both that made it impossible for the marriage to endure.

4. The causes of annulment are rooted in the human dimensions of marriage and include such things as immaturity, emotional illness, addiction, or other behavioral disorders that would make a life together as husband and wife impossible. The process of securing an annulment of a failed Catholic marriage usually begins at the local parish level with an information-gathering procedure. Then Church professionals interview both parties to the marriage. In the United States the processing of cases usually takes about fifteen months; there is no charge connected to the granting of annulments, but those who can make an offering to defray costs are usually asked to donate $250. (About 40 percent of those who obtain annulments pay nothing.)

5. Those who receive an annulment must first obtain a civil divorce. The Catholic Church recognizes both a civil and a religious dimension to the marriage. The civil aspects are resolved by civil divorce (support, custody, and so forth), whereas the religious aspects are resolved by the Church court or Marriage Tribunal. If a marriage is annulled by the Church, any children to such marriage are not illegitimated by the annulment, since legitimacy is a civil concern and is protected by civil law. Further, children in no way are hampered as Catholics by the annulment of their parents' marriage.

6. It is estimated that about 10 percent of divorced Catholics in the United States have received annulments of their failed marriages. Many people choose not to avail themselves of the annulment process; others do not use it because of misunderstanding. The Church does not hold that every failed marriage can be annulled; it distinguishes between those failed marriages that were fatally flawed from

the beginning and those that were stable, healthy unions for many years, but later broke down. Marriages of the second kind cannot be annulled.

7. When Catholics divorce and do not obtain an annulment, they cannot celebrate a second marriage in the Church. The Roman Catholic Church chose some thousand years ago to restrict second marriage as a way of reinforcing the permanence of marriage. The Church's prohibition of second marriage is seen as a kind of deterrent to divorce and as a way of encouraging couples in troubled marriages to exhaust every alternative in resolving marital problems.

8. Catholics in the United States divorce somewhat less than the population at large, yet all evidence suggests that they remarry at ordinary rates. This means that about 75 percent of the divorced eventually remarry. There are, therefore, many Roman Catholics in the United States who have married a second time and have not had their new marriage celebrated in the Church. When divorced Catholics go ahead with such a marriage, they are not penalized in any way. (There was once a Church law in the United States, however, that attached an excommunication to such a second marriage, but it was removed in 1977.) There has been a great deal of misunderstanding in the popular mind on this point. In 1981 Pope John Paul II, in a letter on family life, clarified the situation, insisting that those who have remarried without Church approval remain part of the Catholic community and should be welcomed to participate in the life of their local parishes insofar as they are able. He called upon the Church to show itself a "merciful mother" to such remarried couples.

9. Traditionally, the Church has held that such divorced and remarried persons, who have entered into a second union without the Church's approval, should not receive Communion when attending Mass. This is still the basic norm for such remarried persons. Yet the Church is aware that there are often deeply personal reasons for divorce and remarriage, involving no disrespect for Church teaching or law. Local pastors are advised to enter into confidential dialogue with such remarried couples and to be alert to any excusing circumstances. Today, on a case-by-case basis, such remarried couples often choose to take Communion, with the support of their pastors.

10. The result of these developments over the past ten years has

been the expansion of local services to help divorcing Catholics through the human and spiritual crises that follow upon divorce. Further, the expansion of annulment has enabled more and more persons who never had a Christian marriage to be freed from the obligations of such marriages and, if they choose, to celebrate a second marriage in the Church community. Thus the negative climate that saw so many divorced and remarried Catholics becoming alienated from the Church community has been altered. Even those who choose to remarry without Church permission have been assured that such an action does not separate them from the Church community. They are encouraged to continue to live as Catholics, to raise their children in the Catholic faith, and in some circumstances to receive Communion.

Readiness for Remarriage

James J. Young

I never would have married my husband had he not been granted his annulment, a woman wrote last summer to the "Confidential Chat" column of the Boston Globe. *I am a devout Catholic who believes very much in my religion. . . . Since God gave him the O.K., then I knew it was right for us.*

People who are not Roman Catholics sometimes have a hard time understanding why annulment with subsequent Church celebration of a second marriage is so important to Catholics. Many others, Catholics included, would blanch at the writer's assertion that the annulment of this man's first marriage meant that God was giving "the O.K." to a new marriage.

Most Catholics are raised with a strong sense of membership in a community, reinforced by Catholic education and regular Sunday worship. In this respect they are not unlike Southern Baptists or Michigan Calvinists. For Catholics, celebrating a marriage in a Church ceremony carries with it not only community support and approval, but also the promise of God's blessing. It is because Catholics like to feel that they're squared away with the Church community that so many enter willingly into the time-consuming, difficult process of getting an annulment, a process that takes about fifteen months on average. The Catholic Church blesses only first marriages as a way of reinforcing Jesus' call to permanence in marriage; for that reason, a second marriage after divorce is possible for Catholics only when a prior marriage is annulled . . . when it is judged never to have been a genuine Christian marriage from the beginning.

The Church does not claim that permission to marry again in a Church ceremony implies, as the *Globe* letter-writer seems to suggest, that God is giving the O.K. to the new marriage. We would say that God gives the O.K. to all people when they marry, but that does not mean that the marriage is O.K. In recent years, many Catholics have married a second time after annulment, and quite a few of these marriages have caused concern because they have failed.

For this reason, about twenty Catholic dioceses have initiated programs in second-marriage preparation. These programs acknowledge the fact that freedom to remarry in the Church does not guarantee readiness for remarriage. These new programs vary widely. Some involve a number of sessions in which a remarried couple explore key issues; others use a discussion group format involving experts and remarried persons as resources. All look at issues common to all people marrying—communications, sexuality, finances, children, religion—but recognize that these issues take on a special complexity in a second marriage.

Dr. Robert Garfield of Hahnemann Medical University in Philadelphia has identified four problem areas for couples entering second marriages.

1. *The couple's previous marriages.* Citing evidence that it takes the average person two to four years to work through the grief and other issues that follow a failed marriage, we see many people carrying unresolved feelings of anger and disappointment with them into a second relationship. For a second marriage to work, both partners must be open about the first marriage. They need to achieve a healthy distance from the past and a helpful understanding of what this failed relationship tells them about their strengths and weaknesses.

2. *The period following their marital separation.* There's an old adage that one has to be able to stand alone before one can stand with another person without knocking the other over. A wholesome independence, marked by new skills in successful single living and by a sense of satisfaction in having mastered many tasks of living alone, should be the expected achievement of the period after separation.

3. *The families of origin.* Dr. Jessie Bernard, who studied two thousand remarried people, asserts that family members' acceptance of the divorce and the new partner was the most significant factor in determining the success or failure of a second marriage. Rejection and alienation can be devastating over the long term, and may be difficult to resolve when they are based on unresolved issues of dependency and competition. "You and me against the world" is not a very good way to begin a new marriage; rather, investing in the difficult tasks of reconciliation and mutual acceptance may be important premarital groundwork. Often, clergy can be important allies and intermediaries when parents' rejecting attitudes are clothed in religious language.

4. *The prospective remarriage family.* With 60 percent of divorced parents bringing children into their new marriages, the problems of forming a new family are perhaps the most complex and challenging aspects of remarriage today. Inherited assumptions about family life, new roles, and emotional boundaries and discipline must be explored in advance. A remarrying couple must win the assent of the children they plan to blend into the new family, and this negotiation will require time and patience. Burgeoning literature on the subject and many new organizations are providing sensible advice for these new kinds of families.

All of us working in the Christian churches with divorced and remarrying persons have become convinced that if couples are given good programs to help them evaluate their readiness for remarriage, and if they remarry only after they have given thoughtful consideration to all these difficult issues, then God's blessing may have appropriate human soil in which to take root. There's still a lot of wisdom in the old adage: *God helps those who help themselves.*

Growing Ecumenical Cooperation about Remarriage

James J. Young

Some months ago, an Episcopalian priest and friend, Father Bill Hamilton, asked my advice about a divorced Catholic woman. This woman and her Episcopalian fiancé had come to see him to arrange their marriage. She believed this marriage would excommunicate her from the Catholic Church, since the Church does not allow the divorced to remarry.

She was in love, however, and was willing to risk such a painful separation. Sensing the woman was not well informed about Catholic Church law on divorce and remarriage, Father Hamilton suggested she speak with me. When we met several days later, I discovered, in reviewing the details of her first marriage, that this second marriage would not excommunicate her. What's more, it was possible for her to be married in a Catholic ceremony.

Because she had married the first time in a civil ceremony, the Catholic Church had never accepted her first marriage. (Catholic Church law insists that baptized Catholics are not permitted to marry before a civil magistrate.) Some months later, the couple was married in a Catholic ceremony, with a Catholic priest officiating and Father Hamilton present. Father Hamilton's impulse to check out the woman's Catholic standing with me provided a much more satisfying solution for her marriage. Now she and her new husband are both in good standing in their respective churches.

This ecumenical cooperation works both ways. I have often referred Protestants and Episcopalians to ministers of their own churches when they came to me looking for assistance. Clergy in all churches are learning that we help people best when we help them remain in the churches in which they were raised.

The different churches' approaches to divorce and remarriage are confusing at times. The Catholic Church celebrates second marriage after divorce only when the Church annuls the first marriage. (Annulment is a decision that a failed marriage was doomed from the start and could never have succeeded for life.) The Episcopalian Church and the Protestant churches in general celebrate remarriage after divorce, although the conditions for remarriage may vary with different churches and pastors. For example, an Episcopalian priest must obtain his bishop's permission to perform a second marriage, whereas a Methodist pastor can decide himself whether the couple are ready to be married a second time. In the past, when divorced Roman Catholics were often shunned in their own community, many found comforting pastoral care and help in marrying a second time from Episcopalian and Protestant churches.

Catholics and other Christians are growing in mutual respect for each other's approach to marriage. Today, no church pretends to have worked out perfectly the many complexities of modern marriage. All the churches propose, as Jesus did, that marriage should be a permanent commitment. Ideally, there should be no divorce. Churches have differed for over a thousand years on how to respond to the sad fact of divorce and the human need for remarriage. Historically, the Catholic Church has taken a strict stand on permanence and has tried to reinforce it by being restrictive about remarriage. The Orthodox churches and the churches of the Reformation have been more flexible in permitting remarriage, although they also insist on permanence as a goal.

I remember a case where two divorced Catholic friends who had not received annulments and therefore could not celebrate a second marriage in the Catholic Church decided to marry again in a Protestant ceremony. This couple received fine second-marriage preparation from the officiating minister. I had explained to them the possibility of annulment, but for serious personal reasons they had decided not to avail themselves of this remedy. I told them that if they went ahead with this marriage, they would still be part of the Catholic community. (Prior to 1977, when Pope Paul VI removed the law, the penalty of excommunication was attached to such remarriage.) I shared with this couple a recent statement of Pope John Paul II:

> I earnestly call upon pastors and the whole community to help the divorced [and remarried] and with solicitous care to make sure that they do not consider themselves as separated from the Church, for as baptized persons they can and indeed must share in her life. They should be encouraged to listen to the word of God, to attend the Sacrifice of the Mass, to persevere in prayer, to contribute to works of

charity, and to community efforts on behalf of justice, to bring up their children in the Christian faith, to cultivate the spirit and practice of penance, and thus implore day by day, God's grace. Let the Church pray for them, encourage them and show herself a merciful mother. . . .[1]

Since such remarried Catholics are in a marriage that has not been celebrated in the Catholic Church, the appropriateness of their taking Holy Communion should be discussed with their local priest after the marriage has taken place. The norm of the Church is that such remarried Catholics ordinarily should not receive Communion, since they haven't observed the Church's laws on marriage. Priests, however, can allow for personal circumstances that may open the way for Communion.

All of us in all the Christian churches are learning that ecumenical cooperation can prevent confusion and, sometimes, unnecessary pain at the start of remarriage.

Note

1. "On the Family," #84, *Apostolic Exhortation of His Holiness Pope John Paul II (December 15, 1981) to the Clergy and to the Faithful of the Whole Catholic Church Regarding the Role of the Christian Family in the Modern World.* Published Washington, D.C., Catholic Conference 1982. From *Origins*, Volume 11, #28 and #29, December 24, 1981.

14

My Story

My Story:
When My Stepchildren Disappeared

Christina Mathers

Soon after my second wedding anniversary, my two stepchildren were secretly moved by their mother from upstate New York to California. How a move like that was orchestrated without our knowing has always mystified me, but it was. In fact, we found out about their departure from a friend. One December evening, he casually told my husband that the first grade had held a going-away party that day for my stepdaughter. His message reached us too late for us to do anything. Even if we had had ample warning, we probably would not have been able to stop the move.

The seven- and eight-year-olds who had spent every Tuesday, Thursday, and Sunday at their father's for the last four years were gone. In their place was a San Diego post office box number, with an admonition not to be late with child support payments.

The bad news in my story goes without saying. The good news is that the children, now fifteen and sixteen, live with us today, and this whole experience taught us a lot about *how to get along*.

Anyone who has lost children in this fashion will attest to the fact that the months following their disappearance are very busy ones. Countless hours are spent in consultation with lawyers, detectives, and counselors. While work, school, and anything extracurricular comes to a screeching halt, you are never still. There is always one more thing you can do to try to get your kids back. Everything else in your life seems truly absurd and irrelevant. Children who should be with you are gone; you are obsessed with the loss and with fear about their welfare. You become so singleminded it's a miracle you have a friend left. You become a bore. Sooner or later, your friends begin to let you know that as sorry as they are about what happened, there's nothing they can do. They don't want to hear about it anymore.

Finding my stepchildren took about a month. Then it took several months of fruitless appeals to get them back. As the parent without custody, my husband was powerless to retrieve his son and daughter. Although his legal right to visitation clearly had been interfered with, the law did not want to get involved. The children were not in any imminent danger, so we were advised to leave well enough alone. We were also advised to kidnap them, move to a different state, and adopt new identities.

We had talked to several lawyers before we found one who could really help us. He was a father who had been through an experience similar to ours. He had entirely new advice for us: "Stop thinking about how you're going to win! This is a no-win situation. Regardless of who's right and who's wrong," he said, "you are going to have to learn to work with the kids' mother, or you can kiss the kids goodbye."

The idea of cooperating with the person who had taken his children sounded totally ludicrous to my husband. But at that point there was nothing else to try. We'd run out of options. This one, though it seemed an almost impossible assignment, had the ring of truth to it. In desperation, we began to rethink the past, to put our anger and resentment behind us, and to negotiate.

Having the children for vacations seemed vastly better than not seeing them at all. Living without them for months at a time and sacrificing many extras to afford the cost of flying them across the country were bitter pills to swallow. But there was no middle ground. Our bargaining won us the kids for two months the following summer. A year later, the oldest moved in with us permanently, and several years later the youngest one joined us full time. By then, we had two children of our own.

My husband slowly learned—by practice—to listen to his ex-wife instead of just talking. He experimented with giving her the benefit of the doubt and trying to put himself in her shoes. This was especially hard at first, because he felt so betrayed. The antagonism he still felt from their divorce had to be controlled and subjugated. With time, he got better. Now, he's a pro. If it weren't for the improved relations between him and his former wife, the children would never have been allowed to come live with us. That meant declaring a truce.

Perhaps the kidnapping of these two children couldn't happen now. Shared custody arrangements certainly make it more difficult, and intrastate agreements about family court matters provide some protection. But the very best solution is to work toward peaceful communications between the parents—it's best for everyone concerned.

My Story: Where Is Justice?

Donna Lynn Deeb

My husband and I have four boys. The two oldest live with their mother most of the time, and with us on weekends and holidays. The four boys are brothers—half by blood, but whole in every other sense of the word, from the seventeen-year-old right down to the eight-month-old. They love each other, though they'd rather fight than admit it. We're proud of the harmony in our family unit, especially because the boys have two different mothers.

We live in a two-bedroom apartment: Michael, eight months old; Joey, three years old; Daddy, and I. When fifteen-year-old Steven and seventeen-year-old Phillip come to stay, we number six in the two-bedroom apartment. The boys battle over use of the bedroom; at bedtime, the baby usually wins, while the others camp out in the small square living room.

Quarters are cramped and privacy is a luxury, but we get by. Perhaps one reason we do manage with so little room is that our time together is so brief. Daddy works fifty to sixty hours a week, some nights and some days. I work full time days. With all the time we put into our jobs, money shouldn't be tight, but it always is. Rent goes up every six months, the dentist is threatening to repossess Daddy's teeth, and the Internal Revenue Service is sending us "Third Request" notices.

We feel the need to buy a house, not only for the room, but for the tax write-off, the equity buildup, and the investment value—to secure a future for our family. However, our savings account never seems to grow into a 5 percent down payment. Phillip will be entering college next year, and Steven two years after that. Joey and Michael outgrow their clothes every three months. Somehow, we must become financially stable.

Although Steven and Phillip love us, the penny-pinching life-style of our home makes them somewhat uncomfortable. The transition between our standard of living and the one they enjoy with their mother always confuses them. At home, a maid cooks and cleans their roomy three-bedroom house. They take long vacations—at least two weeks in the winter at their time-share ski resort and two weeks in the summer on a tropical island. They wear pure gold Seiko watches, play games on their home computer, and wear the very latest in teen fashions from expensive department stores.

Their mother is able to provide this pleasant life-style because her debts were dissolved with her alimony settlement (while Daddy struggled beneath the weight of it), and she receives a good salary, a generous expense account, and child support. God bless her—she and her sons are living the American dream.

Meanwhile, Daddy, Michael, Joey, and I get by, usually managing to make ends meet, though barely.

Into our lives comes a lawyer with a Child Support Modification suit. Steven's and Phillip's mother is demanding more money—three times the amount she now receives. A *cost-of-living* increase.

Lawyers tell us:

"First families take priority over second families in the eyes of Georgia judges. First responsibilities first."

"You went into this marriage with your eyes wide open—you knew you had responsibilities."

"Both of your incomes" (Daddy's and mine) "will be taken into consideration."

"The children of your present marriage" (Daddy's and mine) "will not be an issue here. The needs of your first family will take higher priority. The judge will make sure they may continue to live in the manner to which they are accustomed."

"If you can't pay the increase, boy . . . paddle faster."

But I ask you: What happens if we're paddling as fast as we possibly can? The terrifying fact is that the financial condition of the second family is irrelevant. The judge may legally condemn us to poverty, even though we are both working full-time. Daddy's only alternative would be jail, or leading the life of a fugitive.

Neither food stamp nor welfare programs take into consideration the amount of income deducted from a family's pay and given to another family as child support. Even if the *usable* portion of a second family's income falls within qualifying salary ranges, neither government program will recognize that family's needs.

The Internal Revenue Service taxes the second family on the entire amount of the combined salaries without deducting child support. Most college scholarships also record a family's income without regard for the child support paid to another family.

Children of remarried parents are dependent entirely on their parents' income, without the aid of government agencies or scholarship funds, even if a paralyzing portion of that income may not be used for their necessities.

These children are, after all, "second responsibilities."

Judge, I pray, be fair. No more, no less . . . just fair. I pray you see the children . . . *all* of the children. See how they live, where they go, what they wear. Base your decision on reality—on the lives and futures at stake. If you really do see *all* the children born to a parent, and guarantee each of those children a right to survival, fairness will be the outcome in every case.

But to disregard the needs of subsequent families is to blindly punish remarriage. Justice, be not blind!

All men are created equal—aren't they, America? It doesn't matter what race, sex, religion, or age a person is . . . he or she is entitled to equality under the law. Right? To whom one is born, or when, should be of no consequence in the eyes of justice.

Why, then, do the courts of America grant priority to children of one parent, while disregarding the children of another—based only on the fact that one child was born first?

Is that second-born child less American than the first? Is he or she not entitled to equality under the law, especially in vital matters that concern his or her rightful share of parental support?

If all the children born of a father were also born of the same mother, would the attitude "first responsibilities first" still apply, granting legal priority to the oldest over the rights of the youngest? Just because a person is born first, does he or she deserve better legal treatment than those born later? Should a person be discriminated against in the eyes of the law because of who his mother is, or isn't?

Gray areas in the Child Support Modification laws allow gross injustices to be enforced. There are no black and white laws protecting the rights of remarried families. The only way a child is guaranteed legal protection with respect to support is if his parents are divorced.

Punishing marriage and love, preventing equality, discouraging brotherhood, and encouraging divorce . . . America! Are these laws yours?

My Story:
My Role as a Natural Mother and Now as a Stepmother
Mari Ellen Sabol

Much has been written about the feelings, duties, and rights of the woman placed in the role of stepmother, especially when her husband's children visit on weekends and for part of each summer. But what about the role of the natural mother who has carried, borne, and nurtured the babies, and whose instincts will lead her to protect her children with every ounce of strength?

Certainly, having and rearing her children gives the natural mother a feeling of importance. It hurts and troubles her when she discovers that the stepmother is trying to assume the maternal role, to take command, to undertake responsibilities that belong to the real mother.

I have counseled stepmothers who admit their primary reason for taking over the maternal role is that they feel in competition with the natural mother. It may appear that the father is continuing a relationship with his wife through the children. Also, the husband may make the second wife feel that unless she can be a good mother to his children, she will not be acceptable to him.

The stepmother may have misconceived ideas about the natural mother, too. In all probability she has spent many hours listening to her husband describe the various indignities he has suffered at the hands of his former wife. Though her sympathies are naturally with him, the stepmother may find it helpful to understand the difficulties of the first wife. The real mother has a difficult role to play, handling career and home duties on an inadequate income. Most assuredly she does not need any hostility or deliberate attempts to divide family loyalties.

I am a mother who will soon become a stepmother as well. In the light of my own problems, I have given the two relationships much thought. I believe the best role a stepmother can assume is that of a caring friend. She cannot and should not take over the real mother's role. In fact, she should support the mother's viewpoints in every way possible. The real mother's opinions should be considered and her rules and values followed as much as possible. For example, would the real mother consider letting the children see just any movie, regardless of the theme? Let them stay out as long as they liked? Feel free to leave them alone in the house? Permit after-school activities when school grades are not up to par? It is surprising how often a father and a stepmother will permit something the real mother will not. Perhaps they feel the children will *like them better,* but instead it only adds to the children's feelings of insecurity and guilt, as they are inadvertently being asked to divide their loyalties between two parents.

Of course, problems often arise because of the father's attitude. If the stepmother is made to feel that she is being used as a baby-sitter, entertainer, cook, and custodian, she will naturally resent this position.

The present wife should always attempt to cooperate with her husband and his former wife. It is not an easy undertaking, but sincere and honest attempts at cooperation will make it less difficult for all, especially the children. The real mother will surely be pleased that her children are being treated with kindness. The real mother does not want to compete with anyone, but she will protect her children in any way she can from suffering emotional and physical scars.

These are the thoughts I will take with me when I assume my new life. I will consider myself as having temporary care of another woman's children. I hope this woman will approach my children with the same thoughts and kindness.

My Story:
The "Odd Couple" Families
Barbara J. Bryce

It is a good thing that my second husband didn't live a long distance away from me when we were dating. Our daily telephone conversations started anywhere from 8:00 to 10:00 P.M. and lasted from five minutes to four hours (and that's not an exaggeration). We did get to see each other in person long enough for him to propose.

There was much controversy among my daughter and his two daughters and son about our decision to marry. There was arguing, crying, and comments like "You don't care about our feelings." My fiancé and I tried to convince the kids that the merge would be beneficial to all concerned, for many reasons. Not only did we love each other, but we also wanted to help each other's family with whatever problems needed solving. So, despite the children's opposition, we tied the knot on January 2, 1981. To date we not only have solved some of the difficulties, but have created many more.

After we got married, my daughter and I moved into the house where my husband and his three children had been living. The mixed family of six people was like a can of shaken-up beer on top of a hexagon: bubbly and going in six different directions. The result was chaos.

There were differences in religion, economic background, and educational levels. Now that the "odd couple" families were joined, it was difficult for the neat group to cope with the messy crew, and vice versa.

After trying counseling with several different organizations, my husband and I finally threw up our hands and said, "Kids will be kids." We concluded we'd just have to keep from losing our sanity when one of the children did something we didn't like. My husband and I had trouble—and still do—relating to the behavior of the other one's children, plus that of our own. Despite the kids' many unnecessary questions, not to mention their profanity, disrespect, lying, skipping school, indifference to chores, sloppiness, indirect communication, disorganization, and general disobedience, we manage to survive our many frustrations and keep our relationship intact—but only with much patience and understanding.

Another reason we are able to keep our family working as a cohesive unit is that we plan several enjoyable activities together—dinners out, bike riding, sightseeing, visiting with relatives and friends, trips to the beach and other vacation areas.

My husband and I have found that we can't allow everything to get us upset, or we'd go crazy. We just do the best we can in every situation that arises, and end the day with "Good night" and "I love you."

Sources and Resources

Books for Adults

How to Deal with Your Acting Up Teen-Ager—Practical Self-Help for Desperate Parents, by Robert T. Bayard and Jean Bayard. San Jose, CA: The Accord Press, 1981.

How to Win as a Stepfamily, by Emily B. Visher and John S. Visher. New York: Red Dembner Enterprises, 1982.

Making It as a Stepparent: New Roles/New Rules, (updated edition by Claire Berman.) New York: Doubleday, 1986.

Mom's House, Dad's House: Making Shared Custody Work, by Isolina Ricci. New York: Macmillan, 1980.

Remarriage, a Family Affair, by Lillian Messinger. New York: Plenum Press, 1984.

Remarriage—A Guide for Singles, Couples, and Families, by Anne Lorimer and Philip Feldman. Philadelphia: Running Press, 1980.

Sharing Parenthood after Divorce: An Enlightened Custody Guide for Mothers, by Cijii Ware. New York: Viking Press, 1982.

Stepfamilies: A Guide to the Sources and Resources, by Ellen J. Gruber. New York: Garland Publishing, 1986.

The Child Support Survivor's Guide, by Barry T. Schnell. Salem, N.J.: The Consumer Awareness Learning Laboratory, 1984.

The Stepfamily: Living, Loving, and Learning, by Elizabeth Einstein. New York: Macmillan, 1982.

What Am I Doing in a Stepfamily? by Claire Berman. Secaucus, N.J.: Lyle Stuart, 1982.

Books for Children

Daddy's New Baby, by Judith Vigna. Niles, Ill.: Albert Whitman and Company, 1982. Ages 5–8.

In Our House Scott Is My Brother, by C.S. Adler. New York: Macmillan, 1980. Ages 10–15.

No Scarlet Ribbons, by S. Terris. New York: Farrar, Straus, Giroux, 1981. Ages 13+.

She's Not My Real Mother, by Judith Vigna. Chicago: Albert Whitman and Company, 1980. Ages 5–8.

Strangers in the House, by Joan Lingard. New York: Dutton, 1983. Ages 13+.

The Scarecrows, by R. Westall. New York: Greenwillow, 1981. Ages 13+.

What Am I Doing in a Stepfamily? by Claire Berman. Secaucus, N.J.: Lyle Stuart, 1982. Illustrated by Dick Wilson, Ages 6–10.

Where Do I Belong? A Kid's Guide to Stepfamilies, by Buff Bradley. Reading, Mass.: Addison-Wesley, 1982. Ages 9–14.

Your Father's Not Coming Home Anymore, by Michael Jackson. New York: Richard Marek, 1981. Ages 13+.

Newsletters and Bulletins

Effective Parenting. American Guidance Service, Publishers Building, Circle Pines, MN 55014.

Legal Beagle, a Family Law Reform Newsletter. Coalition Organized for Equality, 68 Deering Street, Portland, ME 04101.

Stepfamily Bulletin. Stepfamily Association of America, Inc., 28 Allegheny Avenue, Suite 1307, Towson, MD 21204.

The Family Therapy Networker, 2334 Cedar Lane, Vienna, VA 22180.

Organizations

American Association for Marriage and Family Therapists, 225 Yale Avenue, Claremont, CA 91711. Provides help in finding a therapist.

Center for the Family in Transition, 5725 Paradise Drive, Corte Madera, CA 94925. Provides a wide range of clinical, research, and educational programs for children in families undergoing separation, divorce, or remarriage.

Center for Parenting Studies, Wheelock College, 200 The Riverway, Boston, MA 02215. Provides seminars and publications on parenting for professionals and parents.

Family Resources/Referral Center, National Council on Family Relations, 1219 University Avenue, S.E., Minneapolis, MN 55414. Provides guidance in finding the correct assistance in local areas.

Family Service Association of America, 44 East 23rd Street, New York, NY 10010. Provides guidance in finding the correct assistance in local areas.

Parents without Partners, Inc., 7910 Woodmont Avenue, Bethesda MD 20814. Provides sponsorship for "Education for Remarriage" groups in some local cities.

Second Wives Association of North America (SWAN), Box 978, Station F, Toronto, Ontario, Canada M4Y 2N9. Provides support and information to second wives and their husbands.

Stepfamily Association of America, Inc., 28 Allegheny Avenue, Suite 1307, Towson, MD 21204. Acts as a support network and national advocate for stepparents, remarried parents, and their children. Provides sixty-two chapter groups for support in twenty-eight states.

The Stepfamily Foundation, 333 West End Avenue, New York, NY 10023. Provides information and research on stepfamilies.

Index

Absentee parent. *See* Noncustodial parents
Acceptance of each other, 95
Adams v. *Adams*, 141–144
Adolescent children, 130–132, 134–136
Affection, 96
Alexander, Alice, 151
Alimony and guilt, 38. *See also* Money
Anger, 59–60
Annulment, 178–179, 180–182, 184
Antenuptial agreements, 31–32
Assets in prenuptial contracts, 28–29
Authority, establishment of, 85, 95–96
Automobile in prenuptial contracts, 29

Bank accounts in wills, 35
Baptiste, Jr., David A., 89, 91–94, 171–173
Beck v. *Beck*, 147
Belovitch, Jeanne, 134–136, 149–151
Berman, Claire, 25–27, 45–46, 71–72, 80–82, 107–108, 119–120
Bilbrey, Donna, 7–9, 37–38, 41–42, 98–101, 137–138
Blended family. *See* Stepfamily
Bloomstone, Bernard, 173–175
Bohannen, Paul, 4
Bryce, Barbara J., 194
Buckley Amendment, 162–164

Celebrations, 165–170
Checking accounts in prenuptial contracts, 29
Child Enforcement Act, 149
Child support, 7–8, 139–159; feelings about, 25–27; and guilt, 38; injustice, 189–192; litigation, 149–151, 190–192; mediation, 141–144; payment enforcement programs, 5–7. *See also* Money

Children, 17, 117–120; access to parents, 118–119, 151; adolescent, 130–132, 134–136; feelings of, 121–138; as go-betweens, 153; mutual, 45–46; older, 89, 130–132; in prenuptial contracts, 29; preparation for remarriage, 22; on stepfamilies, 137–138; at weddings, 121–125; weekend, 114–116; in wills, 32–33. *See also* Stepchildren
Christian marriage, 177–185
Christmas, 165–170
Comin, Paula Ripple, 15–17
Communication, 51–54, 84
Competition, 39–41, 76, 83
Cooperation, 80–82, 188
Credit cards in prenuptial contracts, 29
Custody, 139–159; mediation, 146–147
Cyr, Peter, 144–149
Cyr v. *Cyr*, 147

Debts in prenuptial contracts, 29
Deeb, Donna Lynn, 189–192
Denial of feelings, 49–51
Disapproval of stepfamilies, 171–172
Discipline, 111–114; authority, 85, 95–96; stepfathers' role, 85
Divorce; changing patterns of, 4–7, 15; economic issues, 6–7; emotional resolution, 21; personal growth in, 19, 21–22; Roman Catholic Church on, 177–185; social services for, 5

Einstein, Elizabeth, 18–23, 49–51, 57–61, 111–114, 161–163, 167–170
Empathy, 77–78, 87
Employment in prenuptial contracts, 29
England, divorce and remarriage in, 9–10
Expectations, 53–54, 73, 102

Failure of previous marriage and guilt, 47–48
Family Educational Rights and Privacy Act (FERPA), 162–164
Family; normal American style, 1–4; of remarriage, 2–3; stepparents effect on routines of, 75–76
Fathers; expectations of stepmothers, 88–91; noncustodial, 115; substitute, 83; *See also* Noncustodial fathers; Stepfathers; Stepparents
Fear, 58
Feelings, 21, 57–61; denial of, 49–51; guilt, 47–48, 58–59, 85; letting go of, 60–61
Financial responsibility. *See* Alimony; Child support
Flach, Frederic F., 11–14, 43–45, 47–48, 54–57, 83, 88–91, 132–134
Former spouse, 16–17, 29, 54–57
Former wife and second wife, 39–41
Fourteenth amendment, 6
Fourth Annual Stepfamily Conference (Oct. 1985), 134–136
France, divorce and remarriage in, 10
Freed, Doris Jonas, 31–32
Friendship and new marriages, 17
Furniture in prenuptial contracts, 29

Garfield, Helen, 8
Gender differences in life span, 13
Grandchildren at weddings, 121–122
Guilt, 47–48, 58–59, 85

Holidays, 165–170
Homemaking, 97, 107–108, 109–111
Homosexuality, 151
Hostilities in divorce, 56–57
Humor, 97–98

Incest taboo, 85
Insurance in prenuptial contracts, 29
Insurance policy beneficiaries in wills, 35
Interracial marriages, 171–175

Jealousy, 60, 81–82, 121, 132–134
Joint custody, 140–141, 146–147, 150–159; guidelines for, 152–154

Kargman, Marie, 30–41, 51–54, 102–103, 126–130, 141–144

Keshet, Harry, 152
Keshet, Jamie Kelem, 95–98
Kuyper, Neal A., 28, 32–36, 104–106, 109–111, 121–125, 130–132

Legislation to protect families, 6–9
Life cycles and successful marriages, 11–12
Loyalty conflicts, 123–124, 131, 170

Malicious intent, 86–88
Mathers, Christina, 187–189
Mediation, 141–144, 146–147
Messinger, Lillian, 1–4
Mickelson, Jane, 62–68
Minor children in wills, 35
Misunderstandings, 53–54
Money, 29, 189–192; conflicts, 25–27; and stepfathers, 85; and successful joint custody, 155–156. *See also* Alimony; Child support
Mother role, 192–194. *See also* Stepmothers; Stepparents
Multiracial marriages, 171–175
Multireligious marriages, 171–175

National Conference of Commissioners on Uniform State Laws, 31
The Netherlands, divorce and remarriage in, 10
1975 Family Educational Rights and Privacy Act (FERPA), 162–164
Noncustodial fathers, 115, 144–147. *See also* Child support
Noncustodial parents, 117–120, 147–149; child support payments, 149–151; rights of, 144–147; and schools, 163–164. *See also* Child support

"Odd couple" families, 194–195

Pallow-Fleury, Angie, 68–70
Papernow, Patricia L., 73–79, 151–155
Parenting classes, 111–114
Parents in prenuptial contracts, 29
Pension funds in prenuptial contracts, 29
Personal needs in prenuptial contracts, 29–30
Prenuptial contracts, 28–30, 102–103; and wills, 34–35

Prized possessions in wills, 35
Promises in prenuptial contracts, 29

Racial differences, 171–175
Real estate in prenuptial contracts, 28
Reasonable visitation, 145, 151. *See also*
Visitation rights
Reconciliation, 121
Religious differences, 171–175
Religious practices in prenuptial
contracts, 29
Remarriage (Nov. 1984), 39
Remarriage, 13–20; financial concerns in
25–36; life span, effect on, 13;
preparation for, 20–23, 180–182;
property, debts and investment,
disclosure of, 28–30; reasons for,
18–20; rebound, 18–19; Roman
Catholic Church on, 177–185; and
sexual activity, 119; success in,
11–12, 15
Resentment, 60
Richter, Diana, 81–82
Rivalry, 39–41, 76, 83
Roman Catholic Church on divorce and
remarriage, 177–185
Rotenberg, Ernest, 4–7

Sabol, Mari Ellen, 192
Schools; and noncustodial parents,
163–164; and stepfamilies, 161–164
Second families, 2–3; lack of legal
protection, 7–9
Second husband, financial responsibility
for stepchildren, 25–27
Second wife, 37–42; and child support,
25–27; and former wife, 38, 39–41;
needs of husband, 39–40; as
stepmother, 41–42
Sex, 43–45
Sexual feelings in the stepfamily, 91–94,
119–120
Shared custody. *See* Joint custody
Shared parenting, 146–147
Single parent homes, 165–166
Stepchildren; adjustment to moving, 87;
attachment to, 187–189; and
biological children, 84; conflicts
among, 104–105; disrespectful, 86;
effect on marital relationship, 86–88;
expectations of, 104–105; feelings of,
74–75, 100–101, 118; jealousy of,

132–134; loyalty to parents,
123–125, 131; maturing, 105–106;
and stepparents, 86–88, 100–101,
123–125; stigma of, 1; visiting
parents, 135. *See also* Children
Stepfamilies; adolescents on, 134–136;
adjustment of, 2–3, 99–101;
authority, establishment of, 85,
95–96; anonymity of, 98–99;
conflicting interests, 86–88, 117–120;
discipline in, 111–114; identity of,
95–98; importance of couple
relationship, 78–79; in England,
France and the Netherlands, 9–10;
interracial, 10, 171–173; large,
104–106; multireligious, 173–175;
and new homes, 107–108, 109–111;
premarital contracts for, 102–103;
preparation for, 22; and schools,
161–164; sexual feelings in, 91–94,
119–120; shared experiences, 96–97;
strengthening of, 95–120; weekend
children, 114–116. *See also* Child
support; Second families
Stepfathers, role of, 83–85. *See also*
Second husband
Stepmothers, 37–38, 41–42, 192–194;
fathers, expectations of, 88–91. *See
also* Second wife
Stepparents, 71–94; adolescents on, 135;
cooperation with parents, 80–82;
divided loyalties, 88–91; feelings of,
73–79, 86–88, 100–101; role in
discipline, 112–114; and sexual
feelings between stepsiblings, 91–94;
support system for, 77, 79–80; what
to call them, 71–72. *See also* Child
support
Stepparent-stepchildren conflicts, 86–88
Stepsiblings, 91–94; role in family
cohesion, 92; sexual feelings, 91–94,
120
Surnames, 85, 126–130

Teenagers, *See* Adolescents
Terminology, 71–72
Territoriality, 107–108

Unfulfilled need, 86–88
Uniform Antenuptial Agreement Act, 31
Unmarried cohabitation, 151

Vasectomy reversal, 62–70
Visitation rights, 139–159

Wage assignment law, 5
Walker, Kathleen, 155–159
Wardle, Lynn, 149
Weddings, children at, 121–125

Weekend children, 114–116
Weiss, Joan, 114–116, 123–125
Weiss, Robert S., 117–120, 139–141,
  165–167
Wills, 30, 32–36

Young, James J., 177

About the Contributors

DAVID A. BAPTISTE, Jr., Ph.D., is a counseling psychologist and marital therapist at New Mexico State University. He has published many articles about therapy with remarried families and is currently at work coediting a volume about minority families. He is a Fellow of the American Association for Marriage and Family Therapy.

CLAIRE BERMAN, former president of the Stepfamily Association of America, is a journalist and the author of *A Great City for Kids, We Take This Child: A Candid Look at Modern Adoption, Making It as a Stepparent: New Rules*, and *What Am I Doing in a Stepfamily?* She also is the director of public education of Permanent Families for Children, a unit of the Child Welfare League.

DONNA BILBREY is an advocate for parental rights for the noncustodial parent. Having been married three times and divorced twice, Bilbrey speaks and writes from personal experience. She and her husband are founding members of the organization Parents' and Children's Equality of Indiana.

BERNARD BLOOMSTONE, D.D., is a rabbi and the spiritual leader of Sinai Temple in Springfield, Massachusetts. He is also an assistant professor in the Department of Religion at Springfield College.

PAULA RIPPLE COMIN, former executive director of the North American Conference of Separated and Divorced Catholics, is widely known as a speaker at conferences, retreats, and days of recollection throughout North America. She is the author of four books: *Walking with Loneliness, Called to Be Friends, The Pain and the Possibility*, and *Growing Strong at Broken Places*. Her work has been translated into French and German.

PETER CYR, a joint-custodial father, is president of the National Congress for men and former president of the Coalition Organized for Parental Equality. He is editor for *Legal Beagle*, a family law reform newsletter.

ELIZABETH EINSTEIN, a stepchild and twice a stepmother, is author of the award-winning book *The Stepfamily: Living, Loving and Learning* and co-author of *Strengthening Your Stepfamily*, an educational program for stepparents, and *Stepfamily Living*, a series of booklets. A member of the national board of directors of the Stepfamily Association of America, she is the founding editor of that organization's quarterly publication, *Stepfamily Bulletin*.

FREDERIC F. FLACH, M.D., is adjunct associate professor of psychiatry at Cornell University Medical College, and attending psychiatrist at the Payne Whitney Clinic of the New York Hospital and St. Vincent's Hospital and Medical Center of New York. He is author of *A New Marriage, a New Life; The Secret Strength of Depression*; and *Choices: Coping Creatively with Personal Change*.

DORIS JONAS FREED, a practicing attorney, legal author, and lecturer, has devoted nearly ten years to the issues of family law, divorce, child custody, and prenuptial agreements.

MARIE WITKIN KARGMAN, M.A., J.D., is a clinical sociologist, mediator, and specialist in family law, with a career of thirty years in counseling, publishing, and lecturing on the dynamics of family living. She is author of *How to Manage a Marriage*.

JAMIE KELEM KESHET, an MST, Ed.D. candidate, is director of Stepfamily Services at Riverside Family Counseling in Newtonville, Massachusetts, and author of *Love and Power in the Stepfamily* (forthcoming, McGraw-Hill, 1987).

NEAL A. KUYPER is a Presbyterian minister and diplomate in the American Association of Pastoral Counselors, with twenty-five years' experience in marriage and family counseling. He has written several articles about marriage, divorce, and remarriage and has conducted seminars in these three areas in Bellevue, Washington.

LILLIAN MESSINGER is chief social worker at the Social and Community Section of the Clarke Institute of Psychiatry in Toronto, and a lecturer in the Department of Psychiatry at the University of Toronto. She is editor of *Therapy with Remarried Familes* and is a Fellow of the American Association for Marriage and Family Therapy. She is author of *Remarriage, a Family Affair.*

JANE MICKELSON is a freelance writer whose work consists of short stories and nonfiction articles for magazines. She also is a voice-over narrator and regular contributor to *Evening Reading* on KPFA-Radio in northern California.

ANGIE PALLOW-FLEURY, a registered nurse, has worked as a midwife's assistant and childbirth educator. She is currently studying massage therapy.

PATRICIA L. PAPERNOW, Ed.D., is a stepparent, a psychologist, and director of the Charles River Gestalt Center in Cambridge, Massachusetts. She specializes in therapy, consultation, and training for and about stepfamilies. She is at work on a book about the developmental stages of a stepfamily (forthcoming, Garden Press, 1987).

ERNEST ROTENBERG is first judge of the Bristol County Division of the Probate and Family Court Department of the Massachusetts Trial Court. He previously served as assistant district attorney and special assistant attorney general. A trial attorney for twenty-five years, now serving his fourteenth year as a judge, he has devoted those years to the law and domestic relations as a judge, editor, author, and lecturer for the bench and the bar. The author of *Domestic Relations: The Substantive Law* (1984) and over two hundred other publications, Judge Rotenberg also served on the board of the American Bar Association's *Family Law Quarterly.* Judge Rotenberg has taught at the New England Law School and is adjunct professor of law at Suffolk University.

KATHLEEN WALKER is a journalist at *The Ottawa Citizen* in Ontario. During her twelve years with this newspaper, she has served as art editor and assistant living editor.

JOAN WEISS is a clinical social worker who counsels men and women experiencing marital separation, remarriage, and stepfamily problems. She is president of the Greater Boston Chapter of the Stepfamily Association of America.

ROBERT S. WEISS, Ph.D., is professor of sociology at the University of Massachusetts, Boston, and a lecturer at Harvard Medical School. He is the author of several books, including *Loneliness, Marital Separation, Going It Alone,* and, with C. Murray Parkes, *The First Year of Bereavement.* He has published many articles and chapters in books on the issues of divorce, remarriage, and problems of social isolation.

JAMES J. YOUNG, C.S.P., a Roman Catholic priest and rector of St. Paul's College, founded one of the first support groups in the United States for divorced Roman Catholic men and women. A national spokesman for the needs of divorced Catholics, he was instrumental in aiding the passage of a resolution that led to the removal by Pope Paul VI of the penalty of automatic excommunication attached to second marriages in non–Roman Catholic ceremonies. He authored *When You're Divorced and Catholic* and *Divorcing, Believing, Belonging.* The Reverend James J. Young died September 12, 1986.

About the Editor

JEANNE BELOVITCH is a freelance journalist and a teacher of English. She was previously the founder and editor of *Remarriage* newsletter, from which *Making Remarriage Work* evolved; manager of G&R Publications, publisher of *Lab Report for Physicians* and *Remarriage* newsletters; public affairs writer for United Way of Massachusetts Bay; and assistant vice president, sales promotion, for Putnam Fund Distributors. Ms. Belovitch holds a B.S. degree from the Boston University College of Communication.

WIDENER UNIVERSITY
WOLFGRAM
LIBRARY
CHESTER, PA.

FRAMINGHAM STATE COLLEGE

3 3014 00123 8676